Secrets of ZBrush® Experts:
Tips, Techniques, and Insights for Users of All Abilities

Daryl Wise and Marina Anderson

Course Technology PTR

A part of Cengage Learning

COURSE TECHNOLOGY
CENGAGE Learning™

Australia, Brazil, Japan, Korea, Mexico, Singapore, Spain, United Kingdom, United States

COURSE TECHNOLOGY
CENGAGE Learning™

Secrets of ZBrush® Experts: Tips, Techniques, and Insights for Users of All Abilities
Daryl Wise and Marina Anderson

Publisher and General Manager, Course Technology PTR:
Stacy L. Hiquet

Associate Director of Marketing:
Sarah Panella

Manager of Editorial Services:
Heather Talbot

Marketing Manager:
Mark Hughes

Acquisitions Editor:
Heather Hurley

Project/Copy Editor:
Karen A. Gill

Technical Reviewer:
Ramona Lafountain

Interior Layout:
Shawn Morningstar

Cover Designer:
Mike Tanamachi

Indexer:
Broccoli Information Management

Proofreader:
Laura Gabler

Printed in the United States of America
1 2 3 4 5 6 7 13 12 11

Library of Congress Control Number: 2011933242
ISBN-13: 978-1-4354-5897-0
ISBN-10: 1-4354-5897-4

Course Technology, a part of Cengage Learning
20 Channel Center Street
Boston, MA 02210
USA

Cengage Learning is a leading provider of customized learning solutions with office locations around the globe, including Singapore, the United Kingdom, Australia, Mexico, Brazil, and Japan. Locate your local office at: **international.cengage.com/region.**

Cengage Learning products are represented in Canada by Nelson Education, Ltd.

For your lifelong learning solutions, visit **courseptr.com.**

Visit our corporate website at **cengage.com.**

This book is dedicated to all artists and creative individuals,
who make the world a better place to live.

ACKNOWLEDGMENTS

From Daryl Wise

I would like to acknowledge the following individuals who helped make this book possible. First, I need to sincerely thank the amazing, creative, passionate, and talented artists who agreed to participate in this book. This book is all about artists and their art, and I appreciate them taking the time in their busy day to jump through all the hoops to make this book rich, interesting, inspiring, and informative.

Thank you to my friend and book partner, Marina Anderson. She worked long hours and got everything in on time and in good shape for the editors. Her background in computer graphics was a great asset, and I appreciate working with her.

Also, I want to thank the team from Cengage Learning who steered us in the right direction throughout the entire book-writing process. Thank you to acquisitions editor Heather Hurley, who has always supported me and my books; project editor Karen Gill who, with her devotion to the written word, took what was written by me, Marina, and the artists and then molded and sculpted the text like a ZBrush artist to create this amazing book; tech editor Ramona Lafountain, whom we depended on for her ZBrush expertise, and layout editor Shawn Morningstar, whose eye for design and detail always makes my books look good. I always felt that the Cengage Learning team really enjoyed working on this book and "got" what I was trying to present. They are experts and art lovers, too.

And, of course, this book would not be possible without the professional and devoted team at Pixologic. They have created an artist's tool that constantly evolves and gets better with each release, making it a standard in the creative industry. Thank you to Jaime Labelle, Paul Gaboury, Ofer Alon, and the rest of the team!

I am thrilled to have had the opportunity to put this book together!

From Marina Anderson

It's been exciting to work on this book with all the creative people whom I now want to thank. First, I want to thank the artists across the globe who gave their time and generously shared their expertise with all of us in their tutorials within this book and created such outstanding artwork. Their creativity and passion made this book possible.

Second, an enormous thank you to my coauthor, Daryl Wise, for inviting me to be part of this project. He has been amazing to work with, and I have learned so much from him. His vision for this project and the set of books he has been creating puts so much gold dust in one pot.

Third, I want to acknowledge the Cengage Learning book team, who was a pleasure to work with. Thank you to Heather Hurley, who oversaw our work and kept us in line, and Karen Gill, whose unrelenting hard work and sharp eye made sure that our writing was first class. Also, a big shout out to our tech editor, Ramona Lafountain, and to our layout person, Shawn Morningstar. Thank you so much!

Fourth, I really want to thank the Pixologic team for creating ZBrush. They have unleashed a monster package that has enabled and inspired artists and given them the tools to unleash their creativity and skill set. It is an exciting time in the art and digital world. I'm looking forward to all the new art and digital innovations on the way and can't wait to see the work of artists inspired by the contents of this book.

And on a personal note, lots of respect and love to Inge Schaefer, my soul sister; Jeff Cantanhede, my soul prince; and Louis Anderson, my beautiful son. Thank you for all the silly road trips, life adventures, and all your love and support.

I clearly remember the excitement and frustration of reviewing the first version of ZBrush. That must have been almost 15 years or more ago now. I had been sent a copy to review for a leading design magazine. They didn't know what to make of this strange new product. That very first version was a pale reflection of the current one. I described it as a 2.5D painting system. Its performance was truly spectacular, as was the difficulty of using the strange, nonstandard interface. It was a 2D paint program that let you paint with real 3D depth—sort of. The way I described it was painting with toothpaste on the ceiling. Once you were done, you could break off this 3D relief painting, but it had no back to it. It was really just a deep relief painting: 2.5D.

I recall concluding the review enthusiastically. The software was great fun, fast, and novel. Unfortunately, it was a solution looking for a problem; it didn't suit the 2D paint market; it didn't meet the requirements of a 3D paint program. However, the performance was astounding at the time. Later I had the opportunity to meet with its creator, Ofer Alon, and with Jamie Labelle, Pixologic GM, while I was in the U.S. for SIGGRAPH. I was astounded to find that Ofer had written ZBrush all by himself.

Not shy in giving advice, I told Ofer and Jamie that ZBrush wouldn't go anywhere as it was; it solved no one's problems. I told them that they had to go for full 3D painting with output of fully closed 3D meshes that could be imported into standard 3D software. Fortunately, Ofer was up to the challenge—and then some!

Since that first meeting, Ofer and I have stayed in touch, meeting every few years. I was drawn into the 3D and graphics arts industry and was thrilled to see the spectacular success of ZBrush. It became the de facto standard for 3D painting and sculpting. It also consistently pushed the boundary in delivering technical innovation. Even Ofer's unique interface design has grown to be as powerful and novel as the technical capability of the software.

I have been delighted to see the awesome artwork that ZBrush has enabled artists to create. This is the true legacy of ZBrush: almost single-headedly, it has revolutionized 3D sculpting and painting. Now artists can create 3D models that exceed anything possible with physical sculpting tools in the same time.

ZBrush has earned a place in the hall of fame of 3D software and is distinguished with its ability to allow artists to amplify their sculpting and 3D painting skills far beyond what is possible in the physical world.

Dr. Mark Snoswell
President CGSociety
Founder, CGSociety and Ballistic Publishing

For the past 15 years, **Daryl Wise** has worked as owner/operator of StreetWise PR (www.StreetWisePR.com), a public relations and marketing firm near Silicon Valley. Clients include or have included Macworld Expos, the artist Peter Max, HP, Ambient Design, Adesso, Pixelmator, Gluon, and e frontier. He was director of the Santa Cruz Digital Arts Festival for three years and is a member of Cabrillo College's Digital Arts Advisory Committee. He is the author of *Secrets of Poser Experts* and *Secrets of Corel Painter Experts* (Course Technology PTR).

Marina Anderson is a professional computer games and film artist who has been working with CGI for the past 17 years with companies ranging from Virgin Interactive to the Indestructible Production Company at Pinewood Studios in the United Kingdom. Her skill levels and expertise include character creation, texturing, motion capture shoot directing, and key frame animation. You can find her profile and work online at (Marinamation.com).

Cover Artist Credits

Front Cover

Main image: "Cthulhu" by Chris Nichols
"Head of Woman" by Jeremy Engleman
"Ian McShann" by Maarten Verhoeven
"Merc" by Chris Nichols
"Formic-in Progress" by Stefano Dubay
"Dragonage" by Jason Martin

Back Cover

"Showtime Panel" by Mariano Steiner
"Prince" by Christian Fischer

CHAPTER 13: **Stefano Dubay**

Secrets of ZBrush Experts will give you both technical and creative insights into the artistic working processes of some of today's top ZBrush artists.

ZBrush software has been on the market for many years, and some of the experts featured in this book have been using it since it first became available. The collective wisdom and experience of all the artists featured in this book make for a powerful resource and instructional guide. We hope that you will find this book to be not only educational and enjoyable, but inspiring as well.

—Daryl and Marina

What You'll Find in This Book
The concept for this book is to give the reader the feeling of being inside the personal studio of each expert profiled. The chapters are designed as a conversation with the artist about the artist's creative process and his insights. You'll learn answers to important questions and see detailed, step-by-step techniques demonstrated that the artist thought was important. Some techniques have never been seen before. Each chapter features incredible tutorials and artwork relating to ZBrush.

Who This Book Is For
This book was created as a way to help you learn from ZBrush experts, regardless of your skill level. It is for artists, nonartists, and art lovers. It is for not only all ZBrush and other graphics software users—from the beginner to the professional—but traditional artists and those who aspire to become digital artists.

Although this book contains in-depth technical information that is useful for professionals and expert digital artists, it also has simple step-by-step techniques and information that will be useful for hobbyists, novices, and traditional artists looking to explore another medium.

How This Book Is Organized
Each chapter details the professional background of an individual expert and includes techniques, insights, and resources followed by an image gallery highlighting some of the artist's work, both personal and professional.

What's on the Companion Website
You may download the companion website files from www.courseptr.com/downloads. Please note that you will be redirected to the Cengage Learning site.

On the companion website, you will find many items submitted by the ZBrush experts that are useful, educational, and inspiring.

There is a lot of added value on the companion website, such as image galleries, motion graphics, tutorials, favorite Internet links, and free content.

Please remember that the artwork, graphics, content, and tutorials are property of the artist and cannot be reproduced without their express written permission. Any free content included can be used only for noncommercial use, unless specified otherwise or by consent of the artist.

JASON MARTIN

About the Artist

I consider myself both an artist and a craftsman, with a strong drive and dedication to my tasks at hand and a push to bring out the best in each project. I often find inspiration in the oddest of places and try to interpret and incorporate those thoughts into my daily efforts. Currently I am employed as a 3D character artist through Blur Studio in wonderful Venice, California. Over the past four years, I have had the opportunity to work on a range of projects covering game cinematics, ride films, commercials, and everything in between. The scope of these projects has given me the chance to breathe life into a wide order of unique and interesting characters from all walks of life.

Artist's Statement

I take a hands-on approach. I really prefer to jump into a character and get completely enveloped with his or her or its sense of purpose. I like to get to know my characters. Where do they come from? What is their role? The more information I have, the easier it becomes to understand them. These tidbits help spring life into their very being. I enjoy sculpting organics as much as hard surface; they require different sets of disciplines, and both are equally rewarding. I enjoy all aspects of character modeling, from the initial conceptual stage, to craftsmanship, and all the way down to final texturing. I thrive to be creative and try to challenge myself on a daily basis.

"BigDaddy_out."

JASON MARTIN

Techniques

Technique 1: How to Sculpt and Perform Compositing on a Bust Utilizing ZBrush and Photoshop

When I was approached to do something for this book, I actually struggled to think of any clever tricks I use to sculpt in ZBrush. I realized that I truly don't often do anything fancy; I tend to keep it simple. It was then that it hit me—maybe that's exactly what I should share! So I'm going to demonstrate how to quickly sculpt and build form with just a few select brushes and then some basic compositing tricks using some Best Preview Renders (BPRs) and Photoshop. So let's get started on how I made Mr. "Have you seen my jaw?"

First, you are probably wondering what in the heck this is a sculpt of, right? The guy is walleyed and has no jaw! Well, here's the backstory. I was working on an alien head for this, but I randomly stumbled upon a photograph on the ol' Internet of this guy who was arrested in Arizona and had no jaw. I assume his missing jaw was related to cancer, a birth defect, or maybe a tragic hunting accident. Who knows! But I found it down-right intriguing, so I had to bust out a sculpt of this fella.

1. I start with a base mesh. I tend to build up a clean uniform base mesh in XSI. I'm not opposed to ZSpheres; they have their moments, but sometimes they give me wonky geometry, so taking an extra five minutes to bust a simple base out of XSI isn't gonna kill me time wise. See Figure 1.1.

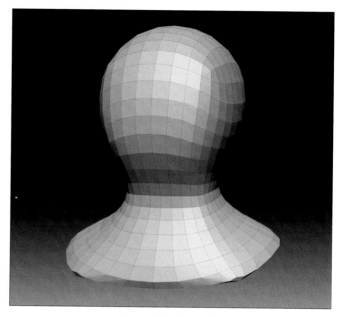

Figure 1.1 Base mesh.

2. The name of the game is to keep things simple, so I use just the following brushes for this bust: Clay Buildup, Clay Tubes, Move Elastic, Dam Standard, and Smooth. See Figure 1.2.

Figure 1.2 Brushes.

3. I go fast and dirty, slapping on form with the Clay Tubes and Clay Buildup Brushes. I want to be loose during this phase, not scared or timid. I focus on laying on form and building up the features and silhouette. I might try out Move Elastic here as well, because it lets me tweak the mesh pretty quickly. There's no reason to go over three subdivisions here; I want it low so it's easy to manipulate and smooth out. I also make sure my brush is set to Symmetry because it makes this phase go that much faster. To activate Brush Symmetry, I choose Transform, Activate Symmetry and then X, Y, or Z. See Figure 1.3.

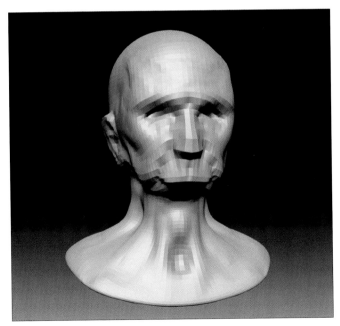

Figure 1.3 Blocking form.

4. Once I have some basic form down, I slap some eyeballs on. These are just placeholders for the time being. In this case, I use two ZBrush spheres. Once I have the base geometry where I need it, I turn off Symmetry. This is where the asymmetry starts to take shape and really breathes life into the character. At this stage, I also subdivide a few more times to be able to get the fidelity I need around the eyes. See Figure 1.4.

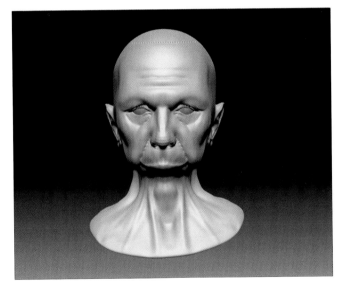

Figure 1.4 Placing eyes.

5. I decide to add a shirt to this guy. The easiest and fastest method to do so is to mask out the area where I want the shirt to be and extract it via the SubTool palette. See Figure 1.5.

Figure 1.5 Extract button.

6. When I click Extract, ZBrush builds a new SubTool of geometry based on my mask selection. Basically, I have a nice form-fitting shirt I can now work with. I adjust the thickness to whatever I need it to be; for this instance, I just leave it at its default setting. See Figure 1.6. Now I have a nice new SubTool to sculpt up the shirt.

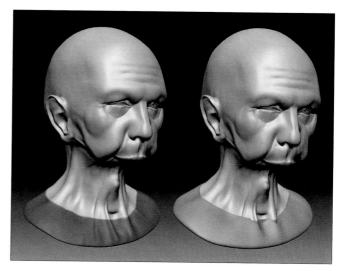

Figure 1.6 Masking and extracting the shirt.

7. Until now, I have only been using the Clay Buildup and Clay Tubes Brushes to build up form and then smooth it out. I'm still primarily going to use those two brushes, but at this point I start to use the Dam Standard Brush to cut in tight creases where I need them. You can see in Figure 1.7 that I have started to build up some wrinkles here and there. I use the Dam Standard to create some of the tighter wrinkles and to cut the creases into the T-shirt. I also take the time to build a simple stand for the bust.

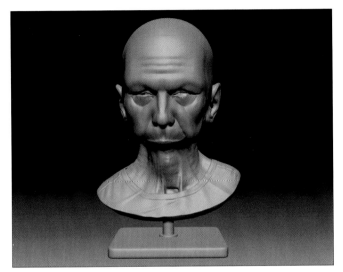

Figure 1.7   Building details.

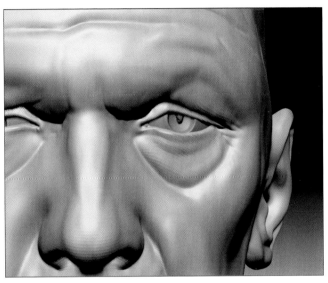

Figure 1.8   Eyes.

8. While I am in XSI, I go ahead and fashion some new eyeballs, too. They are pretty basic; I just add a little wedge to them to give the illusion of reflection. See Figure 1.8.

9. Now that some things are taking shape, I need to figure out how to manage this guy's high-frequency details, such as pores and hair. For the hair, I decide to make a simple custom alpha shape in Photoshop. See Figure 1.9.

TIP

When utilizing alphas, it's always a good idea to subdivide your mesh as high as your PC can handle it. The more sub-divisions you have, the cleaner the alpha looks, so crank it up if you can. (Be careful, though; sometimes if you go too high, your performance is so terrible it may not be worth it.)

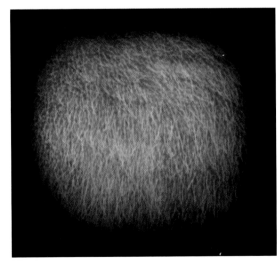

Figure 1.9   Hair alpha.

10. Now I import this PSD file into my alpha menu and apply it using the Standard Brush set to drag rectangle. After I carefully apply it over the scalp, it looks like Figure 1.10. For the pores, I use the variable skin alphas that come with ZBrush. I apply them the same way as the hair, but with a combination of the drag rectangle stroke and the spray stroke. I also add some eyebrows with the Dam Standard Brush. I am getting close to wrapping him up now!

> ## NOTE
>
> You can also download alphas directly from the ZBrush Alpha Library online at www.pixologic.com/zbrush/downloadcenter/alpha.

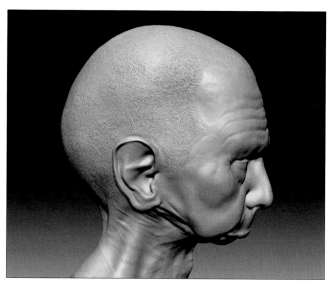

Figure 1.10   Alpha applied to the head.

11. At this point, what's left is pretty much icing on the cake: focusing on the fine details. I really try to sell the wrinkles and pores in this step. Usually after applying pores to the face, I go back through with Clay Tubes, brush at a low setting, and try to add another level of imperfection. This helps break up any monotonous pore patterns and gives the face a more realistic tone. I also decide to take a sec and update the stand. See Figure 1.11. That should do it! Now I composite him.

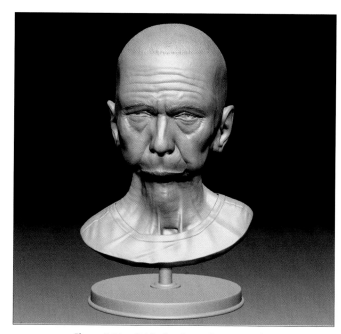

Figure 1.11   Finished sculpt ready to composite.

Technique 2: Simple Compositing Techniques Using BPR and Photoshop

1. Using the same file from Technique 1, I decide to do some BPR renders. I open the Render menu, scroll down, and turn on Render Shadows and AOcclusion. Then I scroll down a little further and expand BPR Shadow and BPR AO (ambient occlusion).

2. Shadows can be adjusted per personal preference. The higher the number, the stronger they are. I tend to set Shadows somewhere in the middle. Because I'm gonna split these into separate passes, I can adjust them to be lighter or darker in Photoshop, so it's not super important to nail it here.

3. I set Rays to 100 for the best quality, and I usually set Resolution to about 2048. Going higher than that is fine, but it takes a little longer to render.

4. I usually leave the Angle alone, but experimentation is fine. Generally, a low number is best for shadows, and a high number like 360 is best for AO.

5. The Blur setting is obvious; the higher the setting, the more your shadows are going to be blurry. The lower the setting, the sharper the shadows.

6. VDepth is an important one. I generally like to set VDepth to −10 and work close to those numbers, because I get way better results.

7. LDepth is something I generally don't adjust.

8. Now onto BPR AO! In this case, I boost my Strength to 1 with the same settings for rays and resolution that the BPR shadow has. I keep the LDepth at −1 and the Gamma at 5.

I want a high Angle so I can get a good occlusion pass, so I keep it at 360. I like the AO pass to be a little fuzzy, so I have it at 8. The Gamma setting is usually good left at 5. It can be adjusted further here for darker AO, but that's not really necessary because it can be tweaked in Photoshop.

Figure 1.12 Setting up BPR.

9. I do one last thing before I click Render. I scroll back to the top of the Render menu and turn on Create Maps. I then click the BPR button and let her rip! Once that's done, in the top of the Render menu under the BPR button are the following passes: Beauty Render, Depth Render, Shadow, AO, and Mask. I leave the Depth settings at default on. See Figure 1.12.

10. In this step, I open Photoshop and import my ZBrush goodness. I use Photoshop CS5 for this, but using a slightly older version wouldn't be much of a hindrance. I open my Beauty pass and duplicate my Shadow and AO pass into separate layers on top of my Beauty. I set them to Multiply and then apply a levels adjustment to both my shadow and AO layers to spice them up a bit. I basically just push up the contrast a tad. I also add a Hue /Saturation level to my Beauty layer. I set it to colorize and tint it a mustard color. See Figure 1.13.

11. It's a good idea to duplicate over the Mask Layer from ZBrush into a new layer on the composition. I use the Magic Wand tool to select the white in the mask and save the selection as a mask. I invert the selection and fill that layer with a green. I then color-correct it with a Hue/Saturation adjustment layer. After that, I import a nice pattern into a new layer and set it to Overlay. I don't want the pattern to cover the bust. I just want it to overlay the pattern on the background, so I mask out that area by using the mask selection. Now, using the same masking techniques, I make two more layers, one with a gradient ramp and one as a drop shadow. See Figure 1.14.

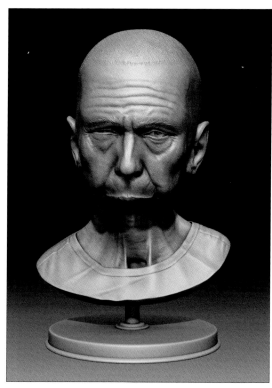

Figure 1.13   Hue/Saturation set to a mustard color.

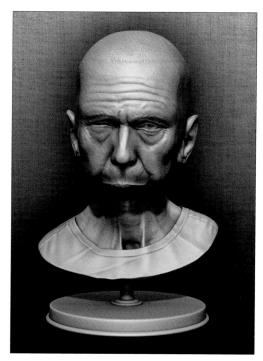

Figure 1.14   Setup backdrop.

12. The background is too uniform in color. I apply two separate Hue/Saturation Adjustment layers to the stack, making sure they aren't set to a specific layer, because I want these applied to the whole image. I tint one layer brown and then fill the mask layer black, hiding the effects. I do the same again but tint it yellow this time. With both layers masked out, I can go to each one individually and paint in subtle color changes a little at a time. On the bottom, I select the Hue/Saturation layer mask to set the color to white. I carefully paint in browns at the bottom and on the other layer do the same but paint in yellows at the top. It's a cool effect! By painting over the bust area, it starts to turn a nice orange brown and gives the bust a nice popping accent. I paint carefully and softly on the left side of the bust to give the appearance of a warm orange casting down the left side of the image. See Figure 1.15.

13. I decide to merge all my layers into a single new layer on top of my stack. With the top layer selected, I go to the menu bar, select Filter, scroll down to Other, and select High Pass. I keep it around the 4–5 range and click OK. The image should be gray and funky looking at this point. When I set this layer to Overlay, *boom!* The image looks a lot different! The High Pass set to Overlay should strengthen all the details. If it's too much, I can dial the Opacity of that layer back to the 60–70 range. See Figure 1.16.

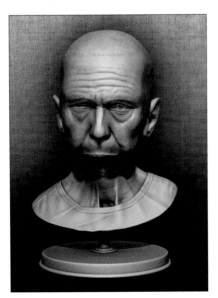

Figure 1.15 Adding color values.

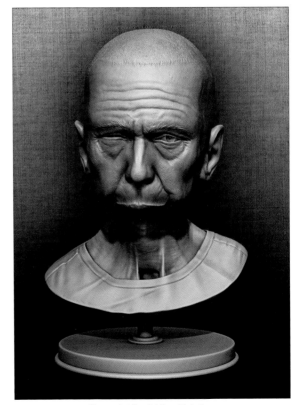

Figure 1.16 Adding High Pass.

TIP

A fast way to merge layers is by creating a new empty layer on the top of the stack and pressing Ctrl+Alt+Shift+E. This merges the stack to one layer and pastes into the layer just created. Everything else remains just the way it was, but there's one condensed layer at the top.

14. The image is looking pretty good now, but I want to break it up a bit more. I set a grunge texture I found to Overlay and place it on top of the stack. Then I mask it out in certain areas so it isn't overbearing. Now is a good time to apply the depth of field look utilizing the depth pass from ZBrush. Again, like I did for the High Pass, I create a new layer on top of the stack and press Ctrl+Alt+Shift+E, pasting the merged image into the new layer at the top. I open my ZDepth pass, select all, and paste it into a new alpha channel of my composition. I then go up to the menu bar and select Filter, Blur, Lens Blur, which opens the Lens Blur settings box. In the top right is a section labeled Depth Map; I click the Source drop-down and select the alpha channel I just made. I then adjust the Radius and Blur Focal Distance until I get the desired depth of field. It really pops the sculpture. See Figure 1.17.

15. I'm pretty happy with what I have, but I still think I could spruce it up a little bit more. I think for this final shot I used the Basic Cool setting in Magic Bullet Looks with an added custom Edge Softness and Vignette. I then do a once-over to see if there is anything standing out that bothers me. I notice that my eye carbuncle is a tad overexaggerated.

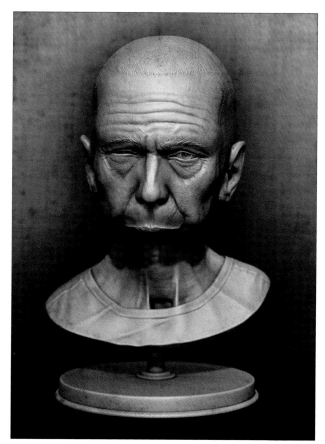

Figure 1.17 Depth of field.

Now instead of going all the way back to the sculpture, I just do a small Liquefy to the image and make sure the area is not so elongated. It's much faster than rerendering everything! There you have it! See Figure 1.18. Also, for reference, I've included a shot of my final composition in Photoshop in Figure 1.19.

TIP

I highly suggest looking into a program called Magic Bullet Looks for step 15. It's a small application that has a ton of predetermined film-like settings you can run an image through to test different looks and feels. This is nothing you can't attain within Photoshop, but Magic Bullet Looks is fast and fun to quickly browse a large range of settings. You can really put the last pass of razzle-dazzle on the image.

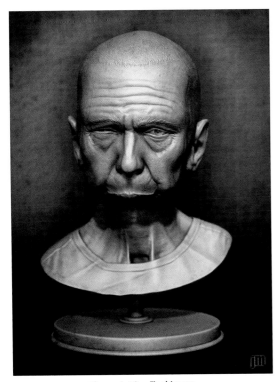

Figure 1.18   Final image.

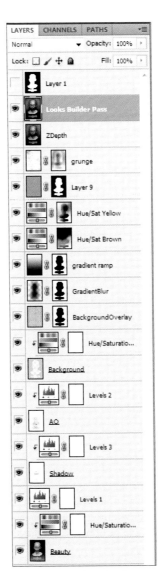

Figure 1.19   Photoshop layers.

JASON MARTIN

JASON MARTIN

Insights

Q&A

What motivates you or your work?

I have a strong inner drive to do the best possible art I can. It's nearly impossible for me to not give 110%. I think a lot of that comes from my loving family. I couldn't do anything if it wasn't for them.

Who/what are your inspirations and influences?

I find inspiration from all sorts of stuff; it's not restricted to the 3D genre. Walking into Blur, I have the opportunity to work with an amazing team of character artists, all of whom have been big inspirations to me and are a helpful set of colleagues. They're a grounded and modest group of good, passionate people.

I find inspiration outside of Blur as well, of course. There are countless modelers, sculptors, and painters out there who drive me. I'm a big fan of the creations of Jordu Schell, Rick Baker, and Stan Winston; their contributions to cinema have been nothing short of incredible. I'm a huge fan of fantasy artist Richard Corben. I love his color palette and paintings. Of course, along with him is the wonderful Frank Frazetta. And Zdzislaw Beksinski has been a great source of inspiration; I can get lost in his paintings! These guys are mentioned often for a good reason: they are amazing at what they do!

I'm a fan of low-brow art as well, from Robert Williams to Robert Crumb and everything in between. Some tattoo artists have made awesome contributions to that scene as well. There is some cool stuff going on there, and not just on skin. A few names that come to mind are Timothy Hoyer, Aaron Coleman, Tim Lehi, and Watson Atkinson.

Also, switching gears back to 3D, it takes only a few minutes at any of the front-runner digital websites like ZBrush Central, 3DTotal, CGHub, and CGTalk to get a good dose of inspiration. I see stuff the younger kids are doing these days, and it's incredible. It's kind of scary to be honest, but it keeps me on my toes! There's so much awesome stuff out there, I can go on for days!

Which artists do you admire? Why?

Mostly I admire the talented modest artists; they are amazing yet have no egos. That can set the most refreshing work environment.

When did you start using ZBrush?

I guess I've been using ZBrush now for about five years.

Describe your creative process and workflow. How does ZBrush fit?

This has changed quite a bit for me over the past two years. I used to use ZBrush primarily at the later stages of modeling, but nowadays I'm in it much earlier on in my workflow.

What are some of your favorite ZBrush features? How do you use them?

I would have to say it's the variety of brushes. There is such an abundance of them that I would be hard-pressed not to find one for any given situation.

Are you using any of the new brushes in ZBrush, like the Move Elastic Brush?

Yes, I've been utilizing all the new Move Brush features as well as all the Polish Brushes. They are a nice addition.

What tools do you most often use to texture? SpotLight? Image Plane? Projection Master? ZAppLink?

ZAppLink is a handy one. I'm constantly using it to stitch and build textures. It's a mainstay add-on I can't live without!

How do you use BPR for rendering out your final image?

I've been using it a bunch lately when I want to be able to present something quickly. It can be a fun way to get something cool for such little effort.

Are you using Photoshop overlay for your final image?

Yes, I believe that's what my technique demonstrates.

Which ZPlugs do you use? How?

SubTool Master, ZAppLink, and Transpose Master are the few I use frequently.

What are your favorite new sculpting tools?

Again, the new brushes are pretty sweet!

What are some of your time-saving tips when using ZBrush on a work project or for personal artwork?

I try to stay in symmetry as much as I can until I get a good solid base form. Once I lock that in, I can go to town with the asymmetry.

Resources

Links

- www.cghub.com
- www.zbrushcentral.com
- www.cgtalk.com
- www.3dtotal.com

JASON MARTIN

Contact

Jason Martin ■ BlurStudio ■ Los Angeles, California, USA ■ nosaj462@gmail.com ■ www.believerdeceiver.com

Education/Experience

Vancouver Film School ■ Degree in 3D animation and VFX, specializing in modeling ■ Art Institute of Las Vegas ■ Bachelor's in media arts and animation

Client List

EA, Namco, BioWare, 2K Games, LucasArts, Capcom, DC, Disney, Avalanche, Pepperidge Farm, Mythic, Rocksteady, High Moon Studios, Bethesda Softworks, Lionhead Studios, Visceral Games

Hardware/Software Used with ZBrush

Hardware: Cintiq with Intel Core i7, 12GB of RAM, Windows 7, GeForce GTX 460

Software: XSI 2012, Photoshop

JASON MARTIN

JASON MARTIN

Gallery

"Brute."

SPLICER BRUTE   BIOSHOCK 2   2K GAMES

BLUR

"BruteCloseUp_out."

JASON MARTIN

JASON MARTIN

HEINRICH   KNIGHTS CONTRACT   BANDAI NAMCO

BLUR

"Heinrich_out2."

"Heinrichcloseup_out."

"Heinrich_ZBrush_comp."

JASON MARTIN

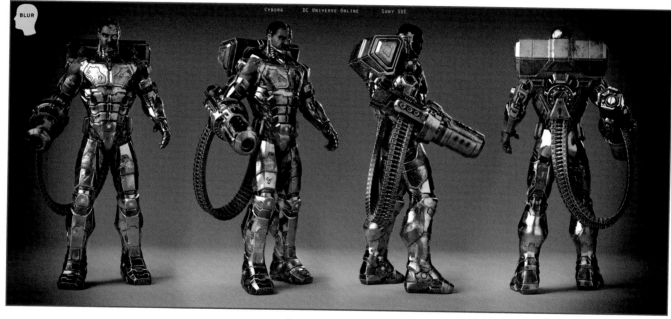

"Cyborg_Zbrush_Comp."

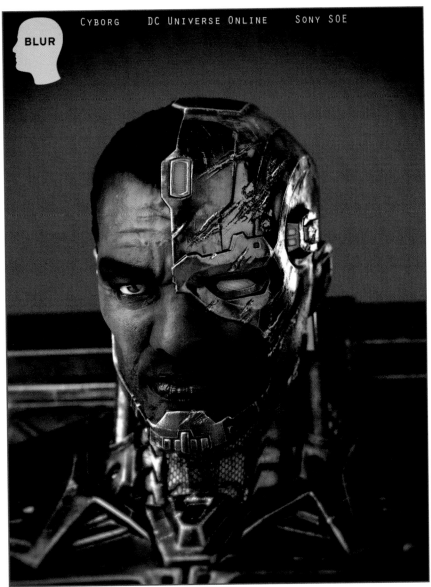

"Cyborg_Closeup."

JASON MARTIN

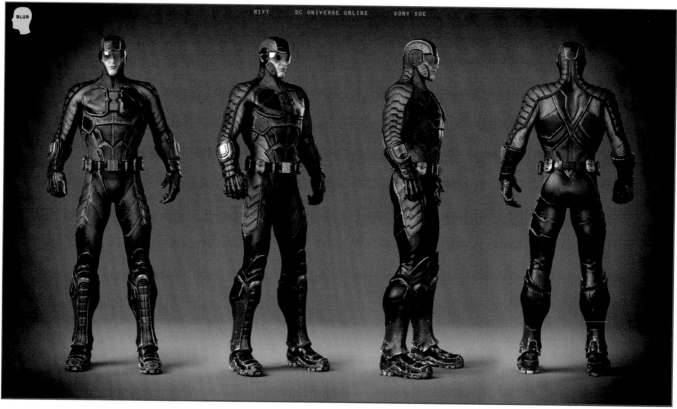

"ShiftComp_out."

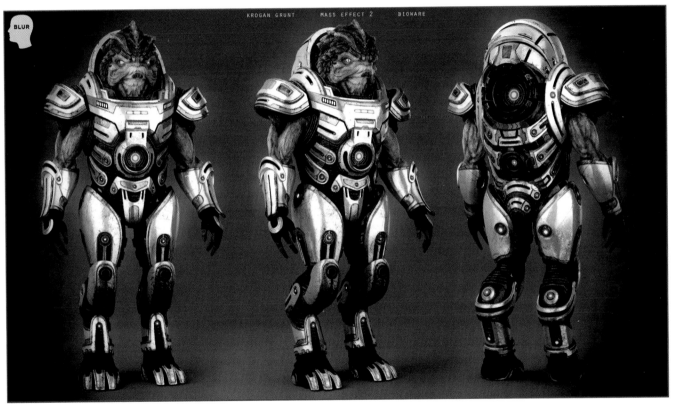

"KroganGrunt_out_out."

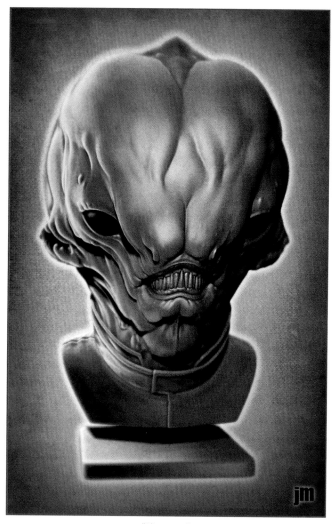

"Alien_out."

"ChompyComp."

MARIANO STEINER

About the Artist

I was born in São Paulo, Brazil, in 1987. I've been a big fan of comics, movies, and games ever since I can remember. Nowadays, as a computer graphics (CG) artist, I see my dreams coming true. I'm passionate about anatomy, which for me is the main goal of any good work. So I always update my studies to grow as an artist. I'm currently employed as a freelance character artist at Tribbo Post, one of the biggest post-production companies in Brazil.

Artist's Statement

A good piece of art is made up of inspiration and devotion. God is in the details! I try to push my limits in every work, improving and testing new techniques and focusing on a good result.

"The Little Monk."

Techniques

Technique 1: The Little Monk

1. The base mesh creation is a simple and quick process. I care more about the structure and the polygon amount on each part than the shape. I need to think where I'm going to include more details and add more ZSpheres to it. I'm careful with weird polygons caused by ZSpheres approximation, because they can ruin the model's symmetry on the next steps. See Figure 2.1.

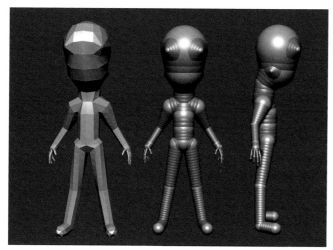

Figure 2.1 Base mesh creation.

2. I block the main shape of my character. I don't care about the polygon count. Using the Move Brush or the new Move Brushes, I reshape my ZSpheres base mesh until I'm satisfied. In this step, I decide all the proportions—cartoony or realistic, human or creature. See Figure 2.2.

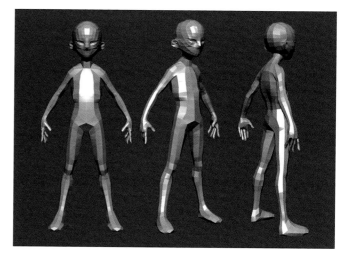

Figure 2.2 Shaping.

3. I block the body anatomy, sculpting the basic muscles and bone shapes. I do it in a simple form, with not too many polygons, just to visualize the body type of my character. The head and the hands have a lot more polygons than the body, because they are the most detailed parts of the model, and the rest will be covered by cloth.

I block the whole body anatomy, even if most of it will be covered by cloth. This way the clothing process becomes a lot easier. I never go too far with this initial anatomy blocking because after the pose I have to resculpt almost everything. In this case, I keep the T-posed model until the fourth subdivision level. See Figures 2.3 and 2.4.

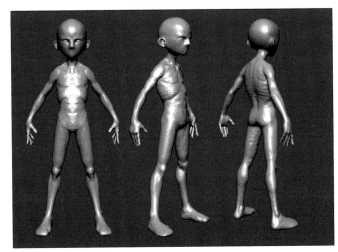

Figure 2.3 Anatomy blocking part 1.

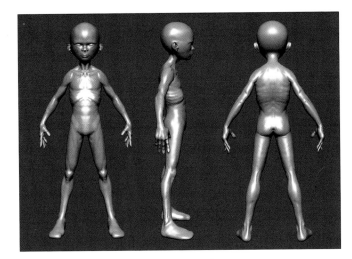

Figure 2.4 Anatomy blocking part 2.

4. I pose my models with Transpose or Transpose Master. This method is not perfect, so I resculpt most of the model here to adjust body distortions, muscle tensions, and so on. I don't go 100% on the anatomy blocking because I don't want to waste work. I search for pose references so I can keep the model's pose realistically balanced. See Figure 2.5.

Figure 2.5 Posing.

5. The last thing I pose in this character is the hands, because I depend on the staff position to do it. I first put the staff in the correct position, and then I adjust the arms and hands to actually grab it, also using Transpose.

After that I refine all the muscles and body shapes to fit the pose and its muscular tension. See Figure 2.6.

MARIANO STEINER

Figure 2.6 Hands posing.

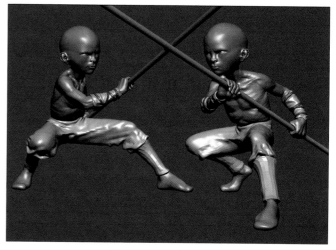

Figure 2.7 Clothing part 1.

6. For this character, I create everything with ZBrush. The Mesh Extraction is a useful tool for this. I just have to mask where I want to put cloth and extract it, like the pants area (mask the legs) or the bracelets fabric (mask the forearm). After extracting the mesh, I inflate it a little bit and then sculpt it as a piece of fabric. I also use ZSpheres to model the "ropes" on the bracelets; then I flatten the surface to look like a fabric strip. With the same process, I create his black belt, the "kimono" suit, and his shoes. For sculpting cloth folds, I mostly use the Standard Brush with LazyMouse and the Slash 2 Brush. See Figures 2.7 and 2.8.

Figure 2.8 Clothing part 2.

7. In this step, I review all the SubTools one by one and refine them, adding more folds on the cloth. With the Rope Brush, I detail the fabric strips on the forearm and legs; force the face expression a bit; add wrinkles, veins, and hair; and work more on the hands. I basically finish the model. I also add a bit of color on the SubTools to make them different from each other. See Figures 2.9 and 2.10.

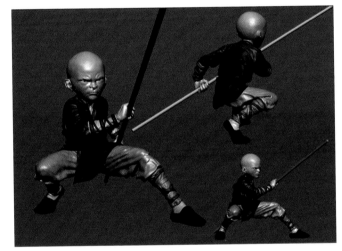

Figure 2.9   Refining part 1.

8. To finish the model, I search for a few alphas on the Internet. Using the ShadowBox feature, I use the alpha in the Mask Brush to create my kung-fu support. No big deal. I just adjust the ShadowBox resolution to 800 instead of 128 (default) so I can get more details from my alpha and make it a polygon mesh. I also add a fabric texture to my cloth using a simple fabric alpha and add the same kung-fu symbol from the pedestal to his back.

Figure 2.10   Refining part 2.

In this case, my initial idea was to do a clay render. But now I start to test some render settings and want to put some color paint on the body. So with the Clay Brush (without Zadd), Color Spray, and a simple dots alpha, I Polypaint the model to create some color variations and make the model look a little bit more real. I don't use ZAppLink or SpotLight to paint with photos because my intention is to create a cartoonish look.

I start to render, with the settings shown in Figure 2.13. For the composing, I take three renders in each position, and each render has a different light direction (main light, fill light, and backlight). After that, I compose the renders in Photoshop, make a few color corrections, and it's done! See Figures 2.11, 2.12, and 2.13.

Figure 2.11 Alpha detailing work and finishing part 1.

Figure 2.12 Alpha detailing work and finishing part 2.

Figure 2.13 Render settings.

Insights

Q&A

What motivates you or your work?

I've always been a big fan of movies and games, so that is my main focus. Being motivated by those is not easy with so many great artists working in this industry. I have to always push my studies further to be able to compete with artists from Pixar, Digital Domain, or Blizzard, for example. This objective is what motivates me to keep moving on.

Who/what are your inspirations and influences?

I take my inspiration from life! Is there anything more inspiring than that? I pay so much attention to everything—from people to buildings—and this gives me many ideas for work. And, of course, I check out forums and artist websites every day.

Which artists do you admire? Why?

They are too many to say. But if I have to say a name, it would be Stan Lee. His work made me what I am today. Stan Lee is one of those amazing guys who can lay down on the bed and think, "Man, I really did something cool with my life."

When did you start using ZBrush?

I started using ZBrush about a year after I started with 3D. I remember being in college when I played with ZBrush for the first time. It was an amazing experience.

Describe your creative process and workflow. How does ZBrush fit?

ZBrush is part of my day. I use it in pretty much every step of my work, from the concept of a character straight through to finalizing.

What's your workflow? Do you create from scratch with ZSpheres or import geometry from another package to work on/develop?

That depends. I do have a few base meshes I use to work, but I usually start from scratch with ZSpheres. It's so much easier to set shapes and proportions with it, and after that I can always retopologize my mesh the way I need it. This way I can free my mind of any restrictions and just let the art flow.

What are some of your favorite ZBrush features? How do you use them?

ZSpheres is the most amazing feature for me. It breaks all the software's technical limitations and lets me sketch anything in just a few minutes.

Are you using ShadowBox to make base meshes? How?

Yes, I am! But I use it mostly for inorganic modeling. It's an amazing tool that makes it a lot easier to model hard edge pieces.

Are you using any of the new brushes in ZBrush, like the Move Elastic Brush?

Yes! Move Elastic and Move Topological are amazing brushes, as are all the Deco Brushes.

What are you using for hard edge modeling?

I'm working a lot with the hPolish and mPolish Brushes because they made hard edge sculpting a lot easier. I also use the new Clip Brushes.

What tools do you most often use to texture? SpotLight? Image Plane? Projection Master? ZAppLink?

I most often use Image Plane and ZAppLink. They are my favorites because they rarely crash or give me any kind of trouble, and they are functional.

MARIANO STEINER

How do you use Best Preview Render (BPR) for rendering out your final image?

I use it a lot now. I like to present my models in clay, so I use a simple setup with strong shadows values, no shadow blur, and two or three different light positions.

Are you using Photoshop overlay for your final image?

Always! I render many passes with ZBrush or any other application so I have better control of my final image. I do main light, backlight, occlusion, depth, lighting, and shadows. With Photoshop, I can blend them and do a fine final composition.

ZBrush lighting is much more complex than ever before. Do you use any of the advanced features? Which ones? Do you use material generating?

I don't take things too far with ZBrush rendering. I do use it for better presentation of my models, but I don't take up too much time setting up a material or a light. I use BPR (Best Preview Render) with shadows, occlusion, and depth. I sometimes use it with SSS (Subsurface scattering), too. But when I have to do something complex, I still prefer to take everything to 3dsMax and render it there.

Which ZPlugs do you use? How?

I use Image Plane a lot at work. Many times I have concept art and I have to make the 3D model exactly like that, so I load the concept as an image plane and sculpt my 3D character with ZSpheres or some base mesh. I also find that the SubTool Master to import new objects, merge, or mirror SubTools is useful. Decimation Master is also part of my day for clay render models approval or simply to reduce the polygon count for retopology.

What are your favorite new sculpting tools?

ShadowBox is an amazing tool that saves a lot of time with inorganic models. The new brushes also make things easier and faster. ZBrush is a complete sculpting software; all that new stuff from now on is just a plus!

How do you use customizable tools in ZBrush?

I don't customize anything on ZBrush. I do everything with what I have, and I think that is enough. The only thing I like to customize is the shaders.

What are some of your time-saving tips when using ZBrush on a work project or for personal artwork?

I always work with the lowest subdivision level possible! I do as much as I can in each subdivision level before dividing the model again. This makes the file faster to work with and with the fewest crash chances. Also, I go for shapes before details. I try to improve the whole shape of a character or an object before I take it to the next level. This way I avoid filling the model with fine details in case I have to go back to redo the shape for any reason and lose all the fine detail work I did.

What advice do you have for artists working with ZBrush?

Anatomy! Always study the anatomy of things, both human and nonhuman. This is what being a great ZBrush artist is all about. The rest is practice and inspiration.

What do you wish someone had told you when you started with ZBrush?

"Forget your characters and creatures for some time, and focus on anatomy studies."

Knowing that can save a lot of time.

How has ZBrush helped you successfully define your own graphic/artistic style?

It has helped with everything, definitely. ZBrush is my main modeling application, and it's where I find myself doing what I like, in the way that I like.

Resources

Links

- www.zbrushcentral.com
- www.cgsociety.org
- http://cghub.com/
- www.3d4all.org/
- www.3dtotal.com
- www.gameartisans.org

MARIANO STEINER

Contact

Mariano Steiner ▪ Tribbo Post ▪ São Paulo, SP, Brazil ▪ marianosteiner@gmail.com ▪ http://msteiner.cgsociety.org ▪ http://mastein3D.blogspot.com

Education/Experience

Graduated with a degree in animation design ▪ Freelance character artist ▪ 3D artist at Tribbo Post and Techno Image

Awards and Career Highlights

CG Choice Award, ZBrush Central Top Row Gallery, ZBrush 4 beta tester, CG Hub Award, CGTalk HCM Challenge Winner, 3D Total Sculpting Challenge Winner

Magazine publications such as 3DArtist, Animation Reporter, Render Out, Sketcher, ZBrush Essentials, Getting Started with ZBrush, and CGWorld

Hardware/Software Used with ZBrush

Hardware: AMD PC, 8GB RAM, ATI Radeon HD 4600 1GB

Software: 3ds Max, TopoGun, Photoshop

MARIANO STEINER

Gallery

"ShowTime strip."

"ShowTime_Front."

MARIANO STEINER

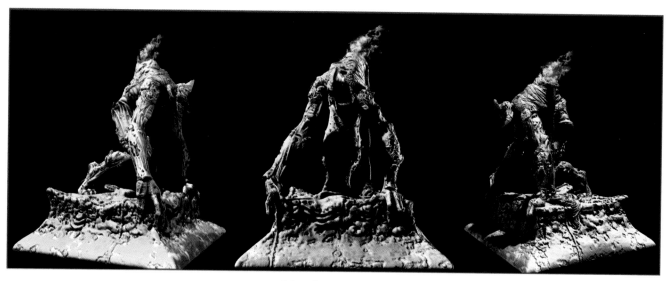

"The Yellowstone Beast."

"Indian Bust."

MARIANO STEINER

"Marvel's Rhino."

MARIANO STEINER

"Comiccon_Agent Zero."

MARIANO STEINER

"Spawn."

MARIANO STEINER

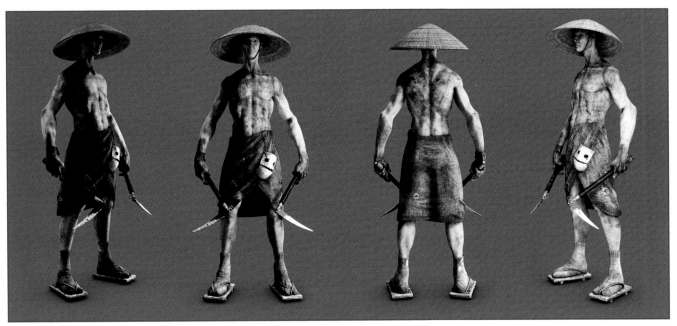

"The Villager_Sample."

"Thor."

"The Mercenary_Front."

CHRISTIAN FISCHER

About the Artist

I have been a character artist working at Crytek in Frankfurt, Germany, for more than two years. Before that, I worked and lived in Hamburg, Germany, where I was born. I have fun modeling humans realistically and testing new 3D tools and workflows. In my spare time, I work on improving my 3D skills, spend time with my girlfriend, and participate in sports.

Artist's Statement

For my work, I try to get as many references as possible. I appreciate valuable feedback from people who know what they are doing. Luckily, I have some great colleagues at work who give me honest feedback. That's the key to getting better.

"Survivor."

Techniques

Technique 1: SpotLight

In ZBrush 4, Pixologic introduced a new Texturing tool called SpotLight.

In this technique, I show a way to texture a head using photo references with the help of some of its features.

1. I load my mesh. It doesn't have to have UV mapping because I will use Polypaint, which stores the color information directly in the polygons of the mesh. To work best, I make sure that I have enough polygons for getting all the information from the texture into the Polypainted head. In my case, the head has around 2 million polygons (see Figure 3.1).

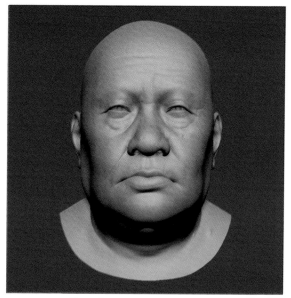

Figure 3.1 Head ready for texturing.

2. In the top menu, I go to Movie, TimeLine, Show to activate the TimeLine in the interface. I rotate my mesh to the front view and set a key by clicking in the TimeLine (see Figure 3.2).

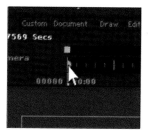

Figure 3.2 TimeLine key for the front view.

3. I repeat step 2 by rotating the mesh to the side view and clicking in the TimeLine again (see Figure 3.3).

Figure 3.3 TimeLine key for the side view.

TIP

It works best for me not to subdivide my mesh too quickly. I always try to get the most out of my mesh before subdividing. That way I'm focusing on the bigger shapes before going into details.

4. Now I can toggle between the different views by using the left and right arrow keys on the keyboard. In this case, I only project the textures from a front and a side view.

TIP

Storing these views is useful because later in the texturing process, you can check the texturing result from all angles and then switch back to the view that matches the actual projection image. You can create as many keys for different views as you need.

5. To be able to paint on the mesh, I activate Colorize under Tool, Polypaint. I select the Standard Brush and make sure that RGB is turned on while Zadd and Zsub are turned off (see Figure 3.4).

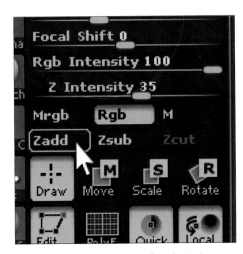

Figure 3.4   Brush settings for Polypainting.

6. I import the photos I want to use for texturing by going to Texture, Import and selecting all the textures I need. After importing, I select the photo from the front and click the right button with the + and – symbol on it (see Figure 3.5).

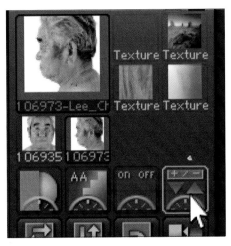

Figure 3.5   Send the image to SpotLight.

7. The image is now active in SpotLight, and a dial contains different tools to manipulate the image in various ways (see Figure 3.6).

8. I switch to my stored front view using the arrow keys and try to match the image as close to the mesh as possible by scaling and rotating it. The Scale Image button is shown in Figure 3.7, and the Rotate Image button is shown in Figure 3.8.

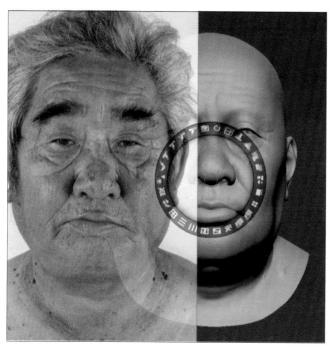

Figure 3.6   SpotLight dial with various tools.

Figure 3.7   Scale Image button.

Figure 3.8   Rotate Image button.

9. I click on the icon and drag left and right. To better see if the texture matches the mesh, I change the Opacity of the photo by clicking and dragging the corresponding button (see Figure 3.9).

Figure 3.9   Opacity button.

Another way to make the texture match the mesh is by using the Nudge Brush. By using this brush, I directly deform the texture (see Figure 3.10).

Figure 3.10   Nudge button.

TIP

For moving the actual SpotLight dial and changing the pivot for scaling and rotating, you can click and drag the orange circle in the middle of the dial.

10. I prefer to match texture and model by deforming the mesh to the texture. For the deformations as well as the Polypaint, I create a new layer under Tool, Layers (see Figure 3.11).

Figure 3.11   New layer for sculpting and painting.

11. I use the Move Brush to match the model to the texture. As soon as I've matched everything, I use the Opacity button to dial down the intensity of the image and press the Z button to hide the SpotLight dial. Now I can paint the texture on the model using the Standard Brush. To check the result, I press Shift+Z to temporarily deactivate SpotLight (see Figure 3.12).

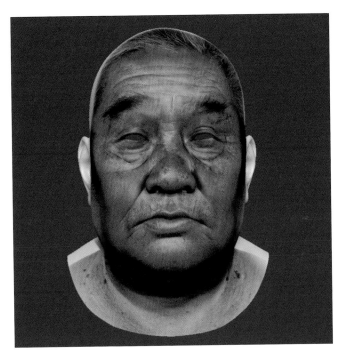

Figure 3.12   Result after applying front projection.

12. I save the actual SpotLight by going to File, Save SpotLight. This is useful for projecting the texture again at a later point because all texture changes and positions are saved within this file.

13. Because I want to get rid of the mesh deformations I did with the Move Brush, I go to the Layers menu, deactivate Record mode by clicking the REC button, and click the Split Layer button (see Figure 3.13).

Figure 3.13   Split layer into two distinct layers for shape and Polypaint.

14. I disable the second layer ending with Shape by clicking the Eye button right next to it. The mesh looks correct again, and the texture still fits.

15. For the side view projection, I repeat steps 5 to 10 with the photo from the side and by using the corresponding stored side view. I also make sure that X Symmetry is switched on to texture both sides of the head simultaneously. I don't care if I paint over the texture I painted from the front because I will erase parts from the side view projection later. Now I have four layers in the Layers menu, of which the two "shape" layers are disabled.

16. I go to the Brush menu, Curve and modify the curve for the Standard Brush as shown. This is important for getting a clean line when erasing color from the side view projection (see Figure 3.14).

Figure 3.14   Modified brush curve.

17. I start erasing color from the side projection by activating Record mode for the layer and holding down the Alt button while painting away areas in the front of the face (see Figure 3.15).

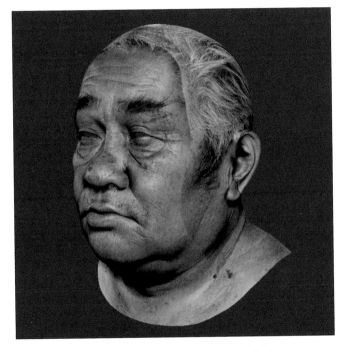

Figure 3.15 Result after applying side projection.

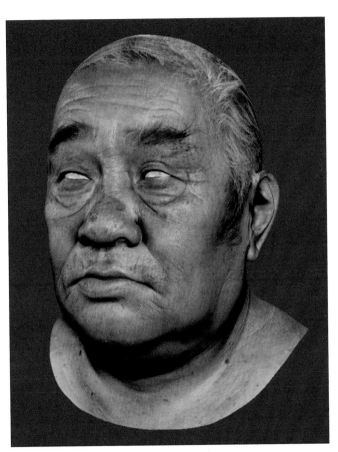

Figure 3.16 Final image.

18. To get rid of the seam, I create another layer, switch back to the stored side view, and activate SpotLight. By lowering the RGB intensity of the Standard Brush to around 15, I paint away those seams and then save my image by clicking on File, Save As (see Figure 3.16).

TIP

By saving the file instead of the tool, you have your time-line views stored in case you want to use the textures later.

CHRISTIAN FISCHER

Insights

Q&A

What motivates you or your work?

What motivates me most is the work of my colleagues. Seeing people ambitious about their work constantly pushes me to give my best. Also, I frequently check different online communities to see what people around the world create. If I see some great sculptures or drawings by other people, it gives me a boost.

Who/what are your inspirations and influences?

I almost exclusively model humans, so reality is my biggest inspiration. It is hard, for example, to make a human face look realistic because people immediately notice anything that is off. I try to get as many references as possible, not only photos but sculpts by other artists I admire and who do their job well.

I also have a big reference folder full of images by classical sculptors. Those old masters were so unbelievably good without all the technology we have today.

What is your workflow?

I often create a simple base mesh in Autodesk Softimage and try to move over to ZBrush as quickly as possible. But this is probably because I'm still so used to creating my base meshes in Softimage. With all the new Mesh Creation tools in ZBrush, I am starting to use ZBrush more to create my base meshes. Because I have to retopologize the high poly models later anyway, I try to spend as little time as possible creating them.

What are some of your favorite ZBrush features? How do you use them?

My favorite feature is masking because it is so intuitive and integrated. If I want to quickly open a mouth, all I have to do is switch to Transpose mode and use auto masking by pressing

Ctrl and dragging onto the mesh to mask the upper lip. Then I can use either the Transpose tools or the Move Brush to modify the lower part of the mouth. Also, I find the auto smooth function of Ctrl-clicking on the mesh or inverting the mask by Ctrl-clicking off the mesh to be very intuitive. Another masking-related feature I frequently use is Mask by Intensity, found under Tool, Masking.

If I have a textured face and want to add pores and small details from the texture, I use the Masking submenu to create a mask based on the texture map applied to the mesh. I can even sharpen the mask and then either use the brushes to sculpt in details where needed or just use Inflat under Tool, Deformation to create irregularities in the skin based on the texture.

Which ZPlugs do you use? How?

The ZPlugs I use most often are Decimation Master for reducing the number of polygons while preserving all the shapes and SubTool Master. SubTool Master is great not only for giving the character a final pose but also for making changes on multiple SubTools at the same time without having to merge them.

What are your favorite sculpting tools?

When it comes to brushes, my favorite one is definitely the Clay Buildup Brush, which is new in ZBrush 4. I also love the different Smoothing Brushes. If I want to smooth out bumps while trying to keep the overall shape, the Smooth Directional Brush is awesome. It is really worth testing all the Smoothing Brushes because some work better in certain occasions than others. There is an alternate Smooth Brush accomplished by holding down the Shift key, clicking on the mesh, and then releasing the Shift key before moving the brush to smooth out the surface.

How do you use customizable tools in ZBrush?

It is great to be able to completely customize the interface to optimize my workflow. I update my interface with tools I use most often and that aren't mapped to hot keys.

I also have a custom menu where I place some frequently used tools that otherwise would be in some submenu spread around the interface.

I have this custom menu mapped to a hot key so that it pops up directly under my mouse when I need it. Macros are another great way to automate almost any task. All those possibilities of modifying ZBrush to my own needs makes it user friendly.

How has ZBrush helped you successfully define your own graphic/artistic style?

Before I used ZBrush, I was concentrating too much on the edgeflow since the wireframe of an object is what you see most of the time. With ZBrush, I focus more on the shapes and then do the topology when the design is finished.

ZBrush even allows me to create a face from a simple box and then later deal with the edgeflow, which is a great advantage.

Resources

Links

- www.zbrushcentral.com
- www.cgfeedback.com
- www.cghub.com
- www.creaturespot.com
- www.cgsociety.org
- www.polycount.com

CHRISTIAN FISCHER

Contact
Christian Fischer ■ Crytek Studio ■ Frankfurt, Germany ■ chris@h3d.de ■ www.h3d.de

Education
Digital Arts Academy AEP ■ Hamburg, Germany ■ 3D Design and Animation

Hardware/Software Used with ZBrush
Hardware: i7 920 PC, 12GB RAM, GeForce GTX 285, Wacom Intuos

Software: Softimage, Mudbox, Photoshop

CHRISTIAN FISCHER

CHRISTIAN FISCHER

Gallery

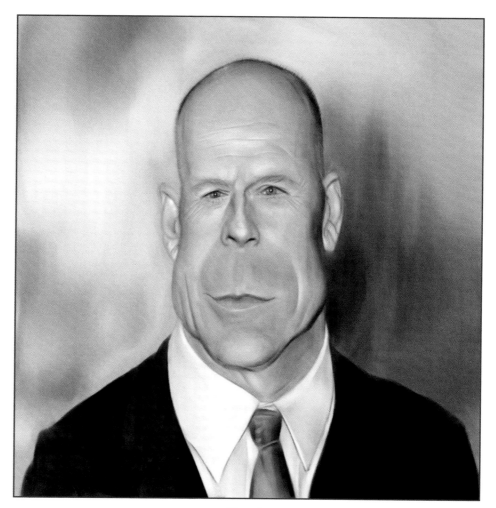

"Bruce."

"Eddie."

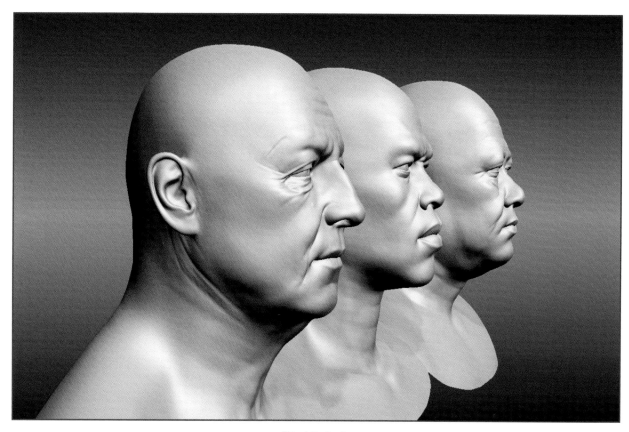

"Head Studies."

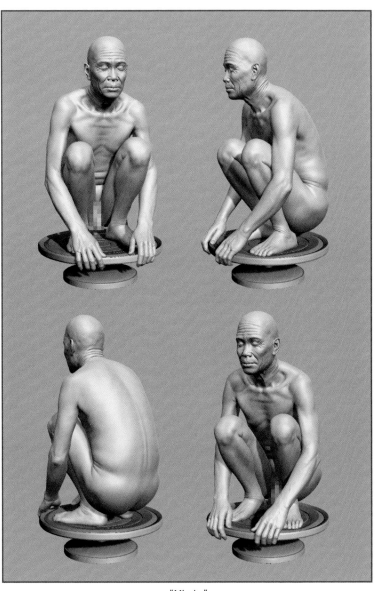

"Minyin."

CHRISTIAN FISCHER

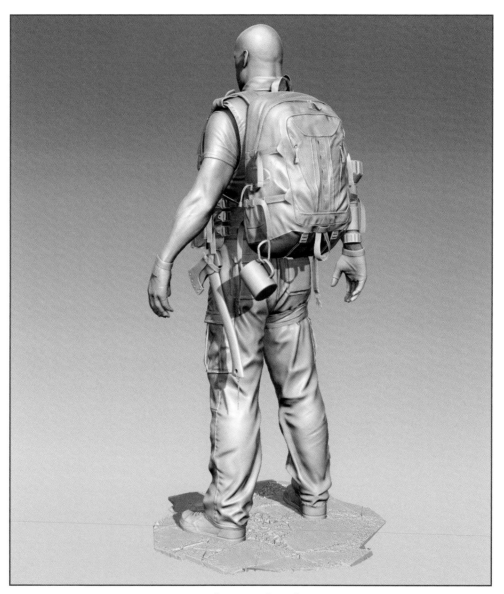

"Survivor-Back View."

"Survivor-Side View."

MAARTEN VERHOEVEN

About the Artist

I'm a Belgium-born computer graphics (CG) artist. I studied classical arts but found my way into the digital realm, with a master's degree in animation. In the past, I've worked as a postproduction artist for color grading and motion graphics for film and commercials. A year ago, I decided to chase my dreams as a CG sculptor and creature designer for toys, film, and games.

Artist's Statement

My personal art is pretty dark for some people, I guess, but I only try to give an alternative vision of the more contemporary creatures. I'm not trying to reinvent the wheel, just trying to dig deeper into anatomy and the older arts by giving them more of a weird personal twist than the average creatures seen these days.

"Gargoyle 07."

MAARTEN VERHOEVEN

Techniques

Technique 1: Keep Detail While Sculpting Using Layers

I use this technique when I need to sculpt cloth and I want to add the flow of the object in the sculpted details. With this workflow, I can keep the added details crisp and still play with the shape.

1. I draw an object on the canvas using a simple plane, but any shape can be used. I ensure the object is subdivided high enough before adding details. Then I go to the main menu and select Tool, which takes me to Menu Dock. I scroll down to the Layers menu above the Geometry menu and click the New layer button. I rename this layer detail. I then click the Record symbol above the slider in the new layer I've just created. See Figure 4.1.

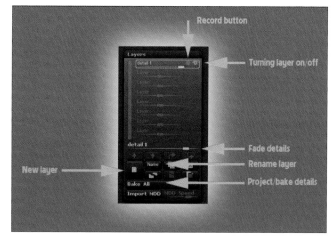

Figure 4.1　Layout of the Layers menu.

2. I import the alpha texture that I want to use as a texture and draw it on my object with the Displace Brush. I create an alpha from an image that I found. See Figure 4.2.

Figure 4.2　Drawing/sculpting the texture on the plane.

NOTE

You can easily download an alpha texture from the Pixologic site (www.pixologic.com/zbrush/downloadcenter/alpha).

3. I click the Record button again in the Detail layer after I have drawn my texture to stop the recording. When I click on the Eye icon, the details should disappear.

4. I start sculpting the extra wrinkles and shapes on the object. The Detail layer cannot be active during this process, so I turn it off and on again. This is important for getting a nice result while adding the wrinkles or folds. See Figure 4.3.

5. When I'm sculpting, I often use a 38 Alpha 38. with the Standard Brush and an Inflat Brush with the gravity turned to 90%. I can change this in the Brush Properties menu under Depth. Then I smooth and polish until I get the shapes I want. During this process, I often go back and forth through the subdivision levels. See Figure 4.4.

Figure 4.3 Turn off a layer's visibility and start sculpting the wrinkles.

Figure 4.4 Keep going over your piece with polish and smooth until you like the wrinkles.

MAARTEN VERHOEVEN

63

6. I go over my sculpts one last time with the Move or Inflat Brush, turning the brush radius draw size to the maximum, and use a low Z intensity. I also start pulling the parts down that are lacking in gravity. See Figure 4.5.

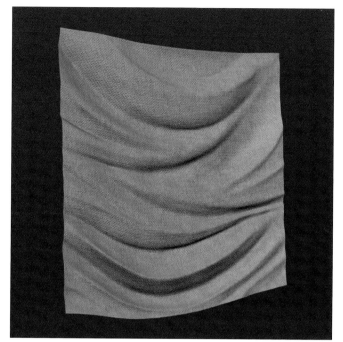

Figure 4.6   Baking in the details of the layer.

Figure 4.5   Adding a gravity pass, and dragging the cloth down with the Move or Inflat Brush.

7. When I'm happy with the results, I click the Bake All button at the bottom of the Layer menu so I can see all the details projected on my object. If I feel that my texture is too strong, I can always use the slider under my Detail layer to dial the details up or down. See Figure 4.6.

NOTE

You can also use this technique in reverse, projecting the details on the master object, but you will lose some details using different brushes like Polish or Clay.

MAARTEN VERHOEVEN

> **TIP**
>
> You can work in several sessions with layers by turning the Record button off and on. You can bake geometry and Polypaint on the model working with layers.

Technique 2: Sculpting Fur with Custom Alpha

Sculpting fur and hair can take a long time. I use this technique for sculpting them easily or to lay out a blueprint for sculpting them. Here I show the basic steps and an alpha to sculpt fur. Knowing these basics allows me to play with the alpha and make it more complex or diverse. See Figure 4.7.

1. I draw an object on the canvas and apply the alpha with the desired intensity at 20% for this demo, using the Displace Brush and DragRect. I can stitch the fur together when I build it in the opposite direction of the hair flow (from the tail to the head). See Figure 4.8.

Figure 4.8   Draw in the fur alpha against the hair flow.

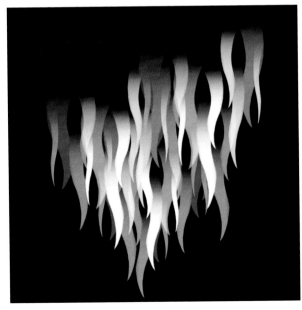

Figure 4.7   Sample alpha.

2. By mirroring and sizing the alpha, I make it feel more randomized. See Figure 4.9.

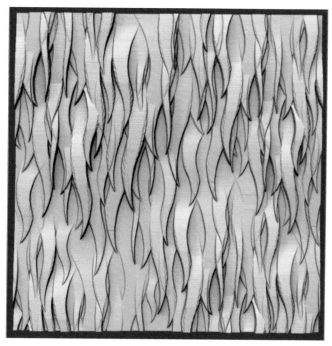

Figure 4.9 Filling in the object.

3. I go over the details and give every hair clump an extra individual thickness using the Clay Buildup Brush first and then polish it with the Smooth and Polish Brushes. See Figure 4.10.

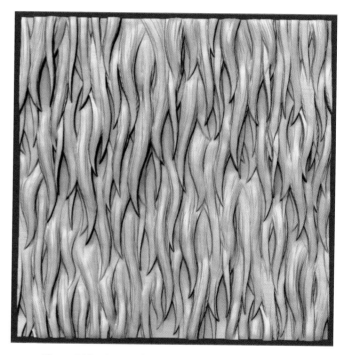

Figure 4.10 Create individual thickness using the Clay Buildup Brush and polish it with Smooth and Polish Brushes.

4. I use the Standard Brush with a 38 Alpha 38. to add an individual pinched/raised highlight in the center of each sculpted clump. See Figure 4.11.

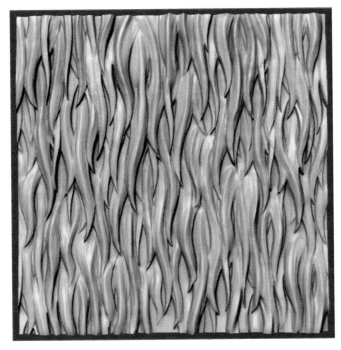

Figure 4.11 Add an individual pinched highlight in the center of each sculpted clump.

5. I tweak the individual clumps using the Move Brush. See Figure 4.12.

Figure 4.12 Tweaking the individual clumps using a Move Brush.

6. Do a final pass of the Standard Brush, with the intensity around 10% using a 59 Alpha 59. to add the strokes of hair. I make sure that LazyMouse is on under the Stroke menu. I turn LazyRadius and LazySmooth to the maximum intensity and LazyStep to the minimum. This way I can easily create smooth strokes. See Figure 4.13.

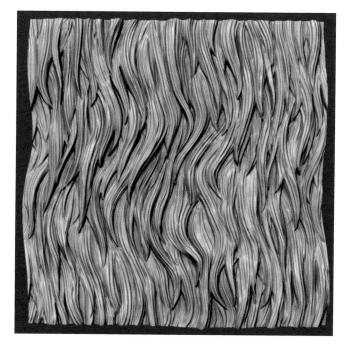

Figure 4.13 A final pass of the Standard Brush and 59 Alpha 59. with LazyBrush on.

Insights

Q&A

What motivates you or your work?

My biggest motivation, however cliché it might sound, is becoming the best artist I can be in my discipline, working with other talented people in the industry, and learning from the masters.

Who/what are your inspirations and influences?

My biggest inspirations and influences are mostly the makeup and VFX artists working for film—those who made my childhood wonderful and fantastic. I'm referring to artists like Dick Smith, Rick Baker, Phil Tippett, and Stan Winston and his crew, to name a few, and not forgetting digital work from companies like ILM, Digital Domain, and many more.

Which artists do you admire? Why?

I admire modern artists who combine crazy ideas with excellent craftsmanship. I also admire the old art masters. Looking at their work in sculpture and paint makes me realize that it isn't so bad studying their work. I find a lot of answers to basic questions regarding form and pose by looking back in history.

When did you start using ZBrush?

I started using ZBrush in early 2009 after seeing some artwork created by Rick Baker, Scott Spencer, Damien Canderle, and Magdalena Dadela. I saw their work, and I was sold!

Describe your creative process and workflow. How does ZBrush fit?

I create most of the creatures in my head and try to give them time to grow. I try to collect as many references during this process as I can, like textures, detailed snapshots of animals, creatures, and people. I use a prebuilt base mesh in ZBrush or build it from ZSpheres, depending on the limbs and proportions of the project. Then I sculpt the creature, pose, texture, and render it in ZBrush. I use the created renders to make a comp in Photoshop.

What are some of your favorite ZBrush features? How do you use them?

I like ShadowBox to build accessories and for my personal work, but also for creating a hard surface for toys. A feature that often helps me is the new Clip Brush and the projection options for transferring details on a new or retopolized surface.

Are you using SpotLight to texture or for sculptural details? Please explain.

I use SpotLight only to paint in textures. It's great to use real photos mixed with Polypaint directly on the sculpt. I can easily correct the images that I want to use by turning the dial for scaling, flipping, and color-correcting my selected image.

Are you using ShadowBox to make base meshes? How?

Yes, I'm using it, but only for props or hard surfaces. They take up too many polygons, and they need to be retopolized if I want a nice polyflow for sculpting. This is of course open for discussion. A good polyflow isn't necessary for sculpting if I'm working on a heavy machine. But when I want to pose my creature and I go into Transpose mode, it doesn't always give a nice clean result in the end.

Are you using any of the new brushes in ZBrush, like the Move Elastic Brush?

I tend to use the Move Elastic Brush when I create fabrics or hanging materials. The two new brushes I use the most are the Clipping Brush and the Move Topological Brush (a big improvement on the Move Brush). It moves only the topology/vertices that are close to the point of movement. When I have a figure with a closed mouth, I can easily pull the lips apart without disturbing the rest of the face.

What tools do you most often use to texture? SpotLight? Image Plane? Projection Master? ZAppLink?

For texturing, I use Polypaint and SpotLight. I've never been a big fan of Projection Master, Image Plane, or ZAppLink. I just love to work directly on the sculpt. The direct interaction with the object is important to me.

How do you use Best Preview Render (BPR) for rendering out your final image?

I use the BPR setting for a few reasons. It gives a real shadow that is easy to tweak, and the ambient occlusion pass is one of the best new additions for final output of my product. It's also nice to adjust the anti-aliasing to create a better image. I haven't used the Subsurface scattering (SSS) setting a lot, but I've seen some nice results from other artists, so it's definitely something I want to check out in the near future.

Are you using Photoshop overlay for your final image?

I use Photoshop for painting and composing my final colored pieces. How I use it differs from image to image. Mostly I render different light settings—top, left, right, and rim—and blend them with a shadow and ambient occlusion (AO) pass. Depending on the material of the skin, I render some material passes and blend them until I get a texture material that I like.

MAARTEN VERHOEVEN

Which ZPlugs do you use? How?

I use SubTool Master a lot for adjusting props and duplicating them, Transpose Master for posing my project with multiple SubTools, and Decimation Master for preparing my mesh for rapid prototyping or KeyShot rendering.

What are your favorite new sculpting tools?

I love to use the new Clay Buildup Brush for blocking out rough shapes quickly. This new tool really speeds up the creative process. It's also great for skin detailing when I use it on a low intensity for building up layers of details.

What are some of your time-saving tips when using ZBrush on a work project or for personal artwork?

Well, that's easy to say when working for someone else. I try to work with enough SubTools and saves during the process so that I'm flexible for adjustments. I use a clean topology for detailing, because it often helps in the end. And I know what I'm going to create, work to a final product, or design even when I'm sketching.

What advice do you have for artists working with ZBrush?

My advice is to learn to see how things work and why they work on a visual basis by studying from the work that's inspiring. Flavors are diverse, and there is a lot of art that can be studied. Also, artists need a talent for real-life sculpting and drawing or a classic background in arts. In the end, ZBrush is a powerful tool that can be mastered to translate art in 3D.

How has ZBrush helped you successfully define your own graphic/artistic style?

ZBrush has helped me become the artist that I am today. I used to work in 3D, but I always found that I was limited in interaction and detailing. The great thing about ZBrush is that regardless of personal sculpting style, I can put my art on the screen in 3D.

Resources

Links

- www.zbrushcentral.com/
- http://cghub.com/
- www.3dtotal.com/

MAARTEN VERHOEVEN

Contact

Maarten Verhoeven ■ Antwerp, Belgium
■ Darth_mutte@yahoo.com ■
http://verhoevenmaarten.blogspot.com

Education/Experience

Master's in animation

I'm working on the Beta team for ZBrush 4.0 and on projects for Hasbro, like the Iron Man, G. I. Joe, and Star Wars toy line. I've received several awards and been interviewed on sites and in magazines including *3Dtotal*, *3Dartist*, *3Dartist Online*, and *3Dcreative*.

Client List

Hasbro Inc., Aaron Sims Company

Hardware/Software Used with ZBrush

Hardware: Two dual, 22-inch widescreen monitors; 9GB of RAM; Intel core i7 920; 2.67GHz; Wacom Intuos 3 A5 special edition

Software: Photoshop

Gallery

"Centaur 03."

"Amazon Crawler 11."

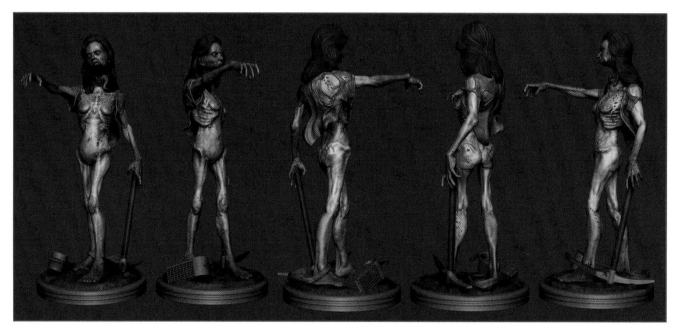

"Banshee Zombie 12."

MAARTEN VERHOEVEN

"Chimp 13."

MAARTEN VERHOEVEN

"Corridorcorpse 06."

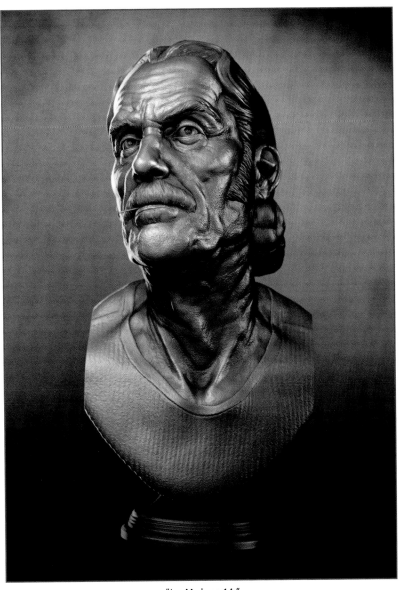

"Ian Mcshane 14."

MAARTEN VERHOEVEN

"Klude 13."

"Master Gorilla King 05."

MAARTEN VERHOEVEN

MAARTEN VERHOEVEN

"Spacepirate 15."

"Trailer Park Queen 04."

http://andbakerdesigns.blogspot.com/

ANDREW BAKER

About the Artist

I am currently a conceptual designer and artist at Weta Workshop design studio in Wellington, New Zealand, where I have been working for more than three years. I studied and received my diploma in design and multimedia and continued on to get my honors degree in computer graphic design, specializing in using 3D software (mainly ZBrush) for character creation. Prior to joining Weta Workshop's design team, I worked at Weta Digital doing previsualization for the upcoming *Tin Tin* film. I have also worked freelance on a couple of video games doing digital sculptures. I have had the pleasure of working on a number of different projects, many of which are still highly confidential. I have been fortunate enough to design some creatures and characters for the upcoming film *The Hobbit*, which is currently in production. Working for great visionaries such as Sir Peter Jackson and Sir Richard Taylor has certainly been a career highlight as an artist.

Artist's Statement

I've always loved the classic painters and sculptors, as well as natural history. I try to apply principles of previous masters. I'm also hugely inspired by evolution. There's such a variety of solutions that nature has provided for inspiration that I'm rarely in a place where I wonder what to paint, draw, or sculpt. It's more the question of "When can I paint or sculpt that?"

"ZBPortrait."

Techniques

Creating Concept Art Using ZBrush

The purpose of this illustration is to highlight my process for creating concept art using ZBrush. There are a lot of techniques out there, and this is by no means the "right" way to do things, but the way I find most efficient. Through my use of ZBrush, my design is able to fulfill a number of the processes a creature or character design will undergo—be it used for concept art, maquetting, rapid prototyping, or passing on to be 3D modeled for animation. I treat my digital sculpt differently, depending on where the design is going. In other words, I sculpt an illustration differently from sculpting for an asset in the film. For this tutorial, I show how I quickly use ZSpheres to sculpt from scratch a character I can use to create a piece of concept art. I also show how I layer those files in Photoshop, and with different layer blending options, begin the process for my painting.

I call this character Bapho. He's a disgruntled Kong-like character who likes waiting in the trees above, where he swings down from those grotesque feet and grabs his victims. I imagined the character as a demon/godlike, gorilla-looking creature, with weird, long hands like feet to offset him slightly and add an element of a somewhat tortured soul. I have him sitting here, worrying his thumb into the last victim's eye. Very grim! With character pieces, I like to get across a sense of history. What has he been doing until this moment, when the viewer comes in? It's not much of a story, but it's enough for me to get this image out and document this process.

I love primates. They're so close to humans with their mannerisms and behavior that they make great subjects to base humanoid characters on. They're not for all briefs, but they were a great source of inspiration for this. However, reference is important. It's why I constantly seek books, documentaries, or imagery of animals, insects, different cultures, different places, the deep sea, and anything out of the ordinary; I never know when it'll come in handy for an idea. I sometimes do studies of my reference as well, to familiarize myself with the forms. This adds to the catalog of things I can draw on for designing creatures and the like.

Technique 1: Sculpting, Posing, and Composition Thoughts

1. For this exercise, I start with ZSpheres and not a generic or imported mesh. I normally make the mesh as simple as I can (and it's always pretty messy!), because I don't know where this character could evolve in the sculpt. See Figure 5.1.

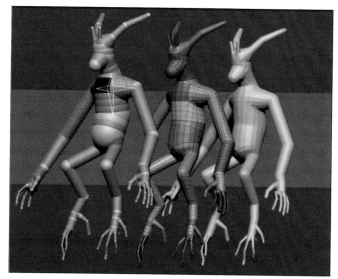

Figure 5.1 The ZSpheres rig created for this character and the mesh it created.

2. The rest of the mesh is relatively simple, but I did have to locally subdivide the face so I could add more information. ZBrush has some great tools for equalizing a mesh. In the Tool menu, under Deformation, I use Relax a lot. I'm also a frequent user of Equalize Surface Area under the Geometry menu. See Figure 5.2.

Figure 5.3 The brushes used to create the forms for a sculpture.

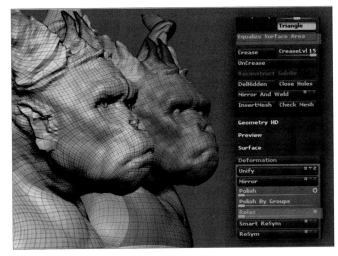

Figure 5.2 The mesh on the right is polygroups from the ZSpheres, and the mesh on the left is polygroups after subdivision and Relax.

3. I generally don't use many brushes. However, I do use Standard, Clay, Clay Buildup, Move, and Inflat for sculpting organic forms. See Figure 5.3.

4. I use some alphas for textural elements when needed. But ZBrush 4 came with a handy function under the Tool menu called Surface. In this menu, there's a great function called Noise. See Figure 5.4.

Figure 5.4 Here the character is masked to show the result of the noise created on the sculpt from the Noise button.

5. Noise allows me to put a general texture pass over the whole sculpt. Most of the time, I know my output will be an A3 size printout and a digital copy of the file viewed on a screen, so I need a fair amount of detail, but not as much as if I were sculpting a character for modeling and animation or 3D output. So for the illustration, I choose carefully where I spend time on detail.

A quick and easy way to add fingernails, horns, or armor into a sculpture is by masking off an area of the character and doing an extraction, which is found in the SubTool menu. That is how I created the fingernails on this character. I find this better than sculpting the fingernails directly into the character. See Figure 5.5.

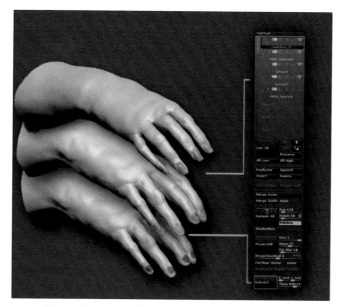

Figure 5.5 Masking the tips of the fingers of the character to extract fingernails.

6. The sculpt took me less than three hours from ZSpheres to posed portrait sculpt. There's a lot I could do at this stage, like take a screen grab of a MatCap gray render, sketch out variations of the character, or add things like jewelry or other props into the scene. But I will do this for the second illustration, where I add a tree and put him in a scene using the same technique. See Figure 5.6.

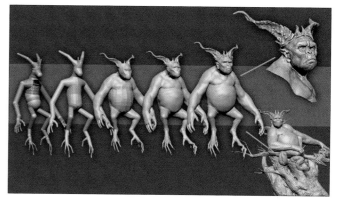

Figure 5.6 The sculpt from ZSpheres to the bust, and the finished design maquette.

Technique 2: Rendering for My Concept Piece

1. ZBrush provides a great toolset for lighting a scene or character. I start with Basic Material 1, which has a diffused highlight. I turn the model to black and turn the background to black so that when I put this to screen in Photoshop, all I'm left with is the highlights. Then I switch to Basic Material 2, which has a bit more of a focused highlight, like for wet or metallic surfaces. I play around with the modifiers in Specular Curve to vary my materials in the scene, and depending on how many materials I have, I create that many different highlight maps. See Figure 5.7.

Figure 5.7 My highlight maps, created by the Basic Materials within ZBrush.

Figure 5.8 BPR render.

2. For shadows, I use BPR (Best Preview Render). I usually render these on the MatCap gray shader. It's lit neutrally, and it works for nearly every image I do. So I render the shadow pass on that shader and put CreateMaps on so I can export those files individually. Normally, I use three or four lights in a scene, but only one or two for shadowing. In this case, I wanted a shadow cast across the character, so I used one light here for that. The rest of the lights are for modeling in the highlights. See Figure 5.8.

Once the render is complete, the maps appear in their respective places.

3. I export a reflection map. I can modify it for my own background to reflect on the model by importing the image as a texture in ZBrush, where I can then apply it to the shader. For this image, I use a texture map that ZBrush supplies.

It pays to play with the reflection pass in Photoshop depending on what kind of surface is being rendered. For skin, I often blur the reflection map and put a noise filter on it, as well as erase areas. Usually I do the eyes separately, because they are a wet surface, and the reflection map can create a great effect on that surface. This really helps when rendering a character in an environment. I also use a MatCap Brown, Bone, and skin for color passes.

4. I then switch from Preview mode to Flat mode to get an alpha channel; while in this mode, I go to Masking and do a Mask by Cavity. This gives me a 2D cavity map to play with. See Figure 5.9.

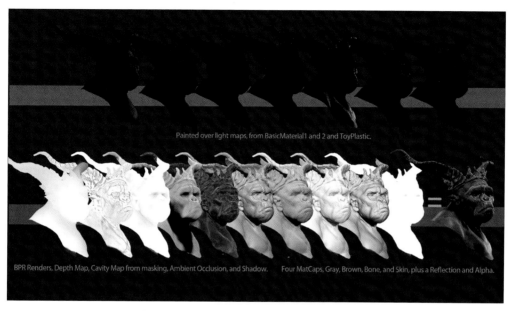

Painted over light maps, from BasicMaterial1 and 2 and ToyPlastic.

BPR Renders, Depth Map, Cavity Map from masking, Ambient Occlusion, and Shadow.   Four MatCaps, Gray, Brown, Bone, and Skin, plus a Reflection and Alpha.

Figure 5.9   All the shaders and renders used from ZBrush.

light_01.PSD
light_02.PSD
light_03.PSD
spec_01.PSD
spec_02.PSD
spec_03.PSD
spec_04.PSD
depth
cavity.PSD
occlusion
shadow
reflection.PSD
Layer 4
colour_01.PSD
colour_02.PSD
colour_03.PSD
alpha.PSD

Figure 5.10   The order in which layers are stacked in Photoshop.

5. Figure 5.10 shows the shaders I used, stacked in the order I would stack them in Photoshop. Light maps are at the top, followed by depth, cavity, shadow, and occlusion, and then my reflection and color maps. It may look like a lot of layers, but the initial control it gives me is great. I often change the color of the maps for various effects.

6. From the top, I apply a Screen mode to all the highlight layers I have in Photoshop. This gets rid of all dark values and keeps the light values on the layer. The advantage to keeping all my lights separate at this stage is that I may want to change the color later. The other layers I apply Screen mode to are the Reflection layer and the Specular layer.

7. I usually change the color of my depth map and apply a Multiply blending option to it. I also change my cavity, occlusion, and shadow, which will be applied as a Multiply blending mode. My gray render is put onto Soft Light (blending mode), giving the dark edges of the piece a little more definition. I put a mask on each of my color layers, and with a soft, white brush in Photoshop, I brush the color back into the image. See Figure 5.11, which shows the layer blending modes used for the various layers.

8. Layering the color shaders like this is much like building a basic SSS (Subsurface scattering) shader. That was my reason for layering them like that. I used to use SSS shaders in Maya a lot, so this method makes sense to me. I treat one color as an Epidermal layer, the next as a Subdermal layer, and the red skin shader as a back scatter. Changing the color of these maps and using the same effect gives me all sorts of cool, translucent, different color skin tones, which is great when I want to show a bunch of options for skin color. See Figure 5.12.

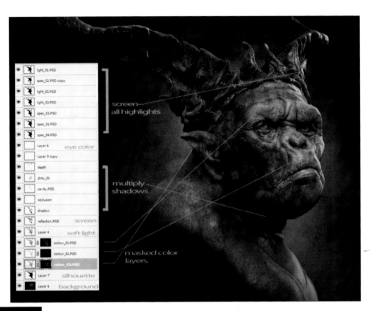

Figure 5.11 A mid-progress shot of the whole piece, taking into account everything rendered from ZBrush as a whole, and using the masked color maps to bring in the color right where it's needed.

Figure 5.12 The final paintup, with Photoshop and ZBrush combined!

NOTE

Know what you're selling. Is it a character? A costume or armor? The answer to this greatly affects how you light, compose, and present your image.

ANDREW BAKER

9. I created a second illustration just to show that putting a character into a scene using the ZBrush model as a base can be a lot of fun. For any project I use a ZBrush base for, the more time I can put into the geometry and sculpt, the more detail I can apply to the image, right up to production quality if that's where I'm going. But it's also great just to explore and see what I can do with the character. See Figure 5.13.

Figure 5.13 Bapho scene.

10. When I think of what pose to create, I sometimes think of what encounter the character will have. Is he in battle? Is he being looked at from below in awe? Has he just spotted something as prey? These sorts of things dictate what pose to go for. It's also tough to judge when to leave sculpting in symmetry and begin on the posed maquette. This varies depending on the level of complexity the design requires. I use Transpose Master a lot for posing my characters, because it allows me to have a number of SubTools and move them around at once.

Here I have used the same method as for the portrait, but I have created a tree and posed the character for this second illustration. Using the same ZBrush model, I'm able to create a few different types of illustrations and potentially export this maquette for 3D output. See Figure 5.14.

Figure 5.14 Pose maquette.

11. I start looking at the character in the angle I'm going to render him in, as well as the space he's sitting in. I put a Basic Material 1 on the sculpt, turning the color to black, and setting my background to black. What I'm doing is checking his highlights. These highlights are going to be what sculpts my form in the 2D image. So I start to play around with a couple of lights to see how he'll be shaped and judge how much information is in those highlights so I know how much more to sculpt for this piece. I also do a quick BPR render with Create Maps on so I can see what the shadows are doing.

I try to think of the composition in triangles, because it targets where I want the eyes to glance over. Here I've drawn over the image to show what I mean. Thinking in triangles also aids in placement of the details. Great designs can be lost when they're not presented well; clients often flip through artwork quickly, so it's important to make the presentation stand out. See Figure 5.15.

TIP

Use Transpose Master to pose characters. It's great for allowing you to have a number of SubTools and still move them around at the same time.

Figure 5.15 Composition.

Insights

Q&A

What motivates you or your work?

I like imagery that tells me a story. So I'm always drawn to character or creature work. The world around me gives me great motivation—people's faces, lives, and stories, or different animals, insects, or other life forms. I like to sit and think what this character does when I'm not drawing it, or what moment I've encountered this creature or character in.

Who/what are your inspirations and influences?

My father and sister are great artists and have been my inspiration to do what I do. I was also hugely inspired by Sir Peter Jackson's *The Lord of the Rings*, and on a daily basis, the team at Weta Workshop, where individuals are an inspiration to each process that is covered.

Which artists do you admire? Why?

I work with a ton of artists who inspire me, including Jamie Beswarick, Greg Broadmore, David Meng, Aaron Beck, Leri Greer, Adam Anderson, and my partner, Lindsey Crummett. The whole team at Weta inspires me. I'm also inspired by the work of Takayuki Takeya, Yasushi Nirasawa, Zdzislaw Beksinski, Wayne Barlowe, John Howe, Alan Lee, and Iain Mccaig. So many inspire me that I can't name each of them.

When did you start using ZBrush?

I believe it was 2003. I came across it while I was doing modeling using Maya at the university. I was drawn to it right away for its ability to handle organic forms without modeling them. Sculpting digitally—it was an exciting thought!

Describe your creative process and workflow. How does ZBrush fit?

On a daily basis, I provide concept art that not only vocalizes an idea but gives a sense of character and is a close representation of what the subject would appear like in the film. It's a tough challenge. I've found that directors quickly try to solve these issues in 3D, be it in clay or ZBrush. ZBrush has allowed me to explore many ideas for illustration purposes, maquette studies, bases for 3D modeling, and even output through milling or rapid prototype. It facilitates the many processes the design is required to go through. That's why I use ZBrush for nearly all my creature or character work.

What's your workflow? Do you create from scratch with ZSpheres or import geometry from another package to work on/develop?

It hugely depends on the brief. I've built a lot of preexisting meshes that come in handy as a base. But sometimes I have to come up with completely different shapes. That's when I use a ZSphere rig, as I did with the illustration for this book.

What are some of your favorite ZBrush features? How do you use them?

BPR is a great feature that gives me accurate maps for rendering illustrations. It's a huge time saver! I also like the Noise feature in the Surface menu, because it gives texture to sculpts.

How are you using TimeLine?

I still need to explore that more!

Are you using ShadowBox to make base meshes? How?

When I do something less organic, ShadowBox helps for little components. But I have not used it to its full potential yet!

Are you using any of the new brushes in ZBrush, like the Move Elastic Brush?

I use some of the planar brushes for doing hard surface, or geometric shapes.

What are you using for hard edge modeling?

I'm using Maya for this.

Are you using ZSketch? How?

Yes, I am. It's great for using symmetry to draw out some quick shapes and ideas if I'm uncertain of where to go in the sculpt.

How do you use BPR for rendering out your final image?

Please reread the "Technique 2" section. I explain it there.

Are you using Photoshop overlay for your final image?

Yes, I use Photoshop for final composite of my illustrations to add a sense of atmosphere and to tighten up the image. I also use it to create variations off one character sometimes, which can be easier in 2D.

ZBrush lighting is much more complex than ever before. Do you use any of the advanced features? Which ones? Material generating?

I generally use the Basic Materials for judging my lighting, as I can modify them to look like any surface. I specifically use them for the highlights. ZBrush also renders out great shadow and occlusion maps through BPR.

Which ZPlugs do you use? How?

I use Transpose Master a lot for combining all my SubTools, getting a little more asymmetry, and posing my characters. In design, we rarely, if ever, show a neutral posed model. I also use Decimation Master for exporting maquettes to be rendered in Maya or exported to the 3D export plug for rapid prototyping.

What are your favorite new sculpting tools?

One of my favorites is Clay Buildup. It's great for blocking out organic forms.

What are some of your time-saving tips when using ZBrush on a work project or for personal artwork?

I find being aware of where the model has to go can save time. If I'm using it for an illustration, I won't get bogged down with too much detail, as I know what the final output will be. Understanding what I want to accomplish and how much detail I want before I start sculpting is a huge help.

What advice do you have for artists working with ZBrush?

It's important to keep learning the fundamentals of art. Software doesn't make someone a better artist. ZBrush has pushed the envelope further regarding what can be created, but having a strong understanding of composition, lighting, and form still makes for better art.

How has ZBrush helped you successfully define your own graphic/artistic style?

It allows me to get that realism I want in my concept art. I can focus strongly on the character and know that when I light and render it, my forms will be accurate to the design.

Resources

Links

Some websites of interest are

- www.physorg.com/
- http://endlessforms.tumblr.com/
- www.escapemotions.com/experiments.html
- http://industrialdecay.blogspot.com/2007_09_01_archive.html
- www.plan59.com/main.htm
- http://digimorph.org/index.phtml
- http://libarynth.org/exoskeletons
- http://philippefaraut.com/portrait.html
- http://nuthinbutmech.blogspot.com/
- www.kenniskennis.com/index2.html

Some artists I've worked with and that are friends, and the Weta website:

- http://skul4aface.blogspot.com/
- http://atanderson.blogspot.com/
- http://benmauro.blogspot.com/
- http://cavematty.blogspot.com/
- http://christianpearce.blogspot.com/
- http://deepcrispyfried.blogspot.com/
- http://crummettcreatures.blogspot.com/
- http://davidmengart.blogspot.com/
- http://frankvictoria-lepicte.blogspot.com/
- http://gregbroadmore.blogspot.com/
- www.john-howe.com/
- www.pushbak.org/
- http://nickbkeller.blogspot.com/
- http://paultobin.blogspot.com/
- http://richypickle.blogspot.com/
- http://crankymachine.blogspot.com/
- www.waynebarlowe.com/
- www.wetanz.com/weta-workshop-services/

ANDREW BAKER

Contact

Andrew Baker ■ Weta Workshop Design Studio ■ Wellington, New Zealand ■ androo.baker@gmail.com ■ www.andbakerdesigns.blogspot.com ■ www.wetanz.com/andrew-baker/

Education/Experience

Bachelor's degree in computer graphic design (Honors)

Awards and Career Highlights

Working as a creature and character designer at Weta Workshop Design Studio, with great visionaries such as Sir Richard Taylor and Sir Peter Jackson. Creating and designing lead creatures for *The Hobbit*. Those have definitely been my highlights so far.

Hardware/Software Used with ZBrush

Hardware: HP workstation, Microsoft Windows XP Professional x64 Edition, an Intel Xeon 2.67GHz CPU, 8GB of RAM

Software: Photoshop, Maya

Gallery

"Ergaster."

"Bapho Scene."

http://andbakerdesigns.blogspot.com/

abaker

"Sculpt Bapho Scene."

ANDREW BAKER

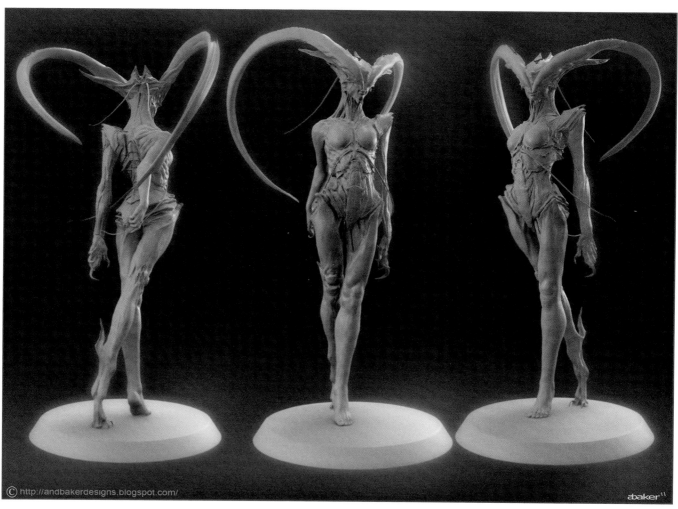

abaker '11

"ZBrush Sculpt Demon."

"Alien 5."

ANDREW BAKER

"The Sik Full Body."

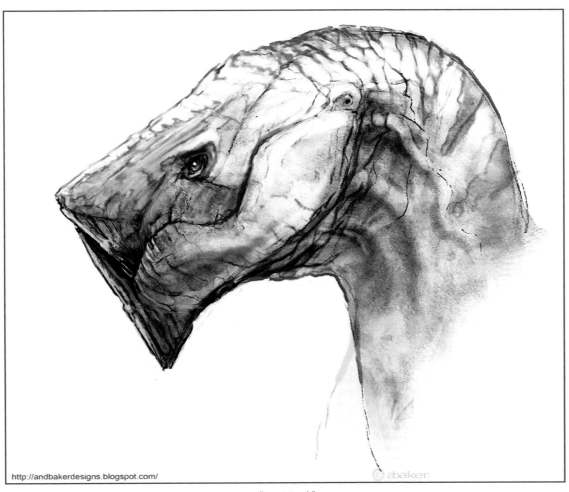

http://andbakerdesigns.blogspot.com/

"Beast Head."

ANDREW BAKER

"Demon Sketch."

© http://andbakerdesigns.blogspot.com/

"Manifest."

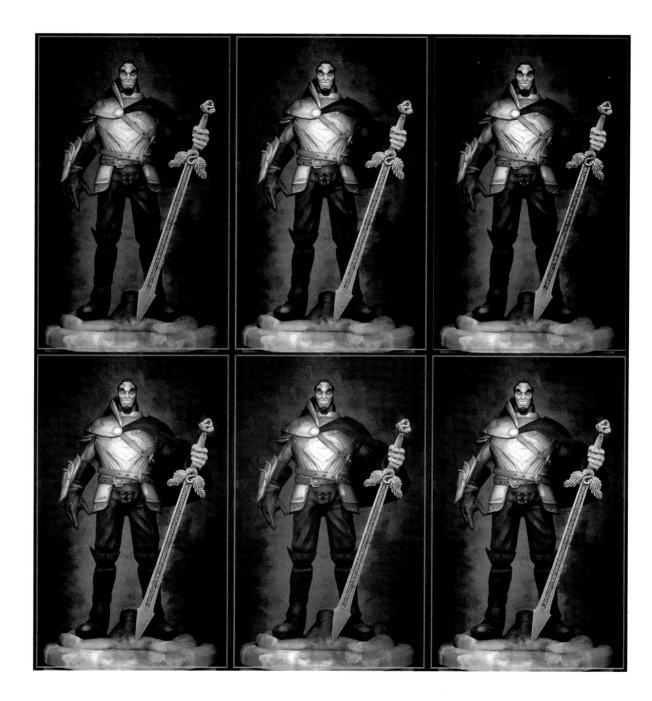

CHAPTER 3

KRISTIAN E DAVIDSON

About the Artist

I'm a character artist working in video games. It's taken me a long time to be able to say that. After studying game design, I, along with a few friends, founded Waking Games in the hopes of turning our shared passion into a shared reality. But as is unfortunately too often the case, this proved a difficult task, and we were forced to put that dream away for later. After that I was able to take a few small projects while working a day job to pay the bills, but it wasn't until I really started getting into ZBrush (with the release of version 3.1) that I started to get noticed. Since being invited to the closed beta for version 4, I've been able to secure a full-time position as a character artist, and I wouldn't have it any other way.

Artist's Statement

I don't know if I'd go as far as saying I have an art philosophy. I suppose a few of the things that really matter to me are a sense of a character having character even when it's just in the default T-pose. Another is that functionality is every bit as important as form. It drives me crazy whenever I see a cool armor design full of curly spiky bits that sure looks intimidating, but you can tell the wearer is going to end up impaling himself if he tries to move at all. I'm also bugged by super-suits that have highly detailed and intricate muscle structure that don't actually account for having a body inside of them. That's about as much philosophy as you'll get out of me.

"KED_PrinceFinalColourComp."

KRISTIAN E DAVIDSON

Techniques

Technique 1: Creating an Epic Sword with ZSpheres and Clay

For this tutorial, I'm going to go over the process of creating a sword almost entirely within ZBrush. The design I'm going with is something I created a while ago, but with this process there's absolutely no reason I couldn't just make up most of it as I go along and still get great results. Due to the way ZBrush currently handles mirroring, I'll be creating only one side of the sword during this tutorial and then welding a flipped version at the end.

1. To start with, I set up a simple chain of ZSpheres in the shape of the sword. Using the lowest resolution of adaptive skin to keep the geometry light, I then use GoZ to bring the mesh into Maya for some quick retopology and adjustments to the geometry. See Figure 6.1.

2. Having fixed up a few odd corners and evened out the polygon distribution, I use GoZ again to bring the mesh back into ZBrush, where I set up some quick Polygroups for later on. I don't need anything fancy here, so I just break it up by the main pieces. See Figure 6.2.

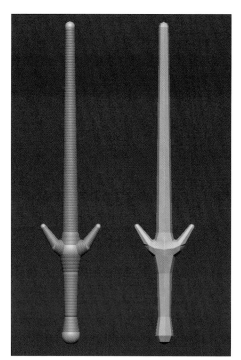

Figure 6.1   ZSphere setup and preview.

Figure 6.2   Low-poly sword base.

3. Using the Move tool and X symmetry, I can begin to add some more shape to the base mesh, adjusting the length of the blade and pulling out the hilt. The design I'm using calls for a swan motif, so I'll be referring to the hilt as the wings from here on. I can now add the first subdivision increase. I turn off Smt for this first increase so that I don't lose the sharp edge of the blade. I use the Clay Tubes Brush to begin adding mass and some basic detail to the swan's body. I can continue to subdivide the mesh as the amount of detail requires, but I sculpt as much as I can on the lower levels first to prevent the "blobby" look. See Figure 6.3.

TIP

If you find it hard to get a readable shape for the body, feel free to turn Smt back on and move up to sublevel 2 to get better control of the details you're sculpting. (The Smt [smooth on or off] button is located within the Geometry menu.)

4. I use dm_standard Brush with default settings (this is the one I load from ZStartup/BrushPresets, not the one already loaded in ZBrush) for narrow, deep cuts like the feathers and the shape of the head. I also use the Move tool to pull out the tips of the feathers, giving them a bit more shape and adding to the overall silhouette. For the leather effect of the hilt, I simply go over it lightly with the Snakeskin Brush. The wraps, which I've decided against, are simple Clay Tubes. See Figure 6.4.

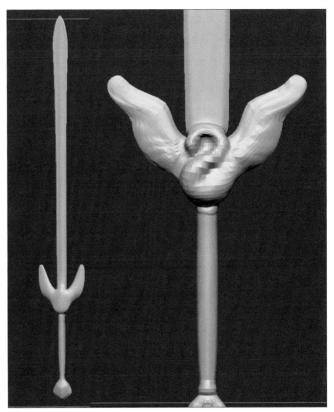

Figure 6.3 Clay sculpting base design.

TIP

If you would like to add the wraps to your own model, you can quite easily sculpt the shapes with Clay Tubes and then refine with the Flatten Brush.

KRISTIAN E DAVIDSON

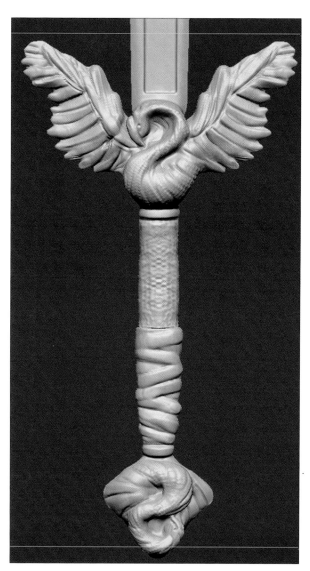

Figure 6.4 Detailing the guard and hilt.

5. To create the indent in the blade and some fancy engraving, I begin by masking off the area to be affected and then using the Deformation menu. I start with a soft mask and inflat at –4; then I sharpen the mask once and inflat –1. I move down to a low subdivision level like 1 or 2 to smooth out the transition at the tip of the blade. I move back up one subdivision at a time while smoothing to ensure a clean transition. See Figure 6.5.

Figure 6.5 Defining the blade.

6. Using the same mask and loading Alpha mm_tatoo04 (available from the ZBrushCentral Alpha Library) on the standard brush, I lower the Z intensity and DragRect across the blade to create a carved engraving pattern. I like mm_tatoo04 because it crosses over itself well, and I can get some unique patterns out of it. See Figure 6.6.

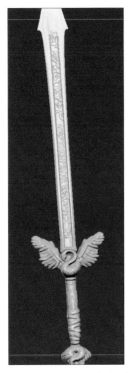

Figure 6.6   Engraving the blade.

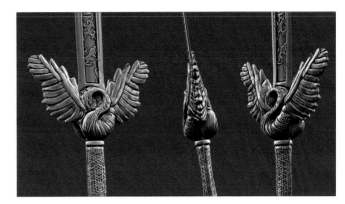

Figure 6.7   Using MatCaps to enhance the details.

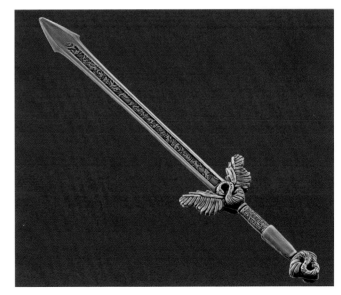

Figure 6.8   The final sword.

7. At this point, I continue to refine the detail and shape of the blade until I achieve a level that suits my needs. See Figure 6.7.

8. The sword I've sculpted is intended to be transferred into a real-time model, so I only need the one side I've sculpted for baking my Normal maps. For presentation purposes, I've made a quick mirror and weld within ZBrush to show the full sword, mirroring one side in −x to create the swan head facing the opposite direction. I've also changed the active MatCap to accentuate the details. See Figure 6.8.

Technique 2: Rendering a Final Image with BPR and Photoshop

For this tutorial, I go over the process I've developed using ZBrush Best Preview Render (BPR) along with Photoshop to create my final "Karloff the Uncanny" image.

1. Through a fair bit of trial and error, I've come to use render settings highlighted in Figure 6.9. I take four separate BPR renders using the following materials: mt_Fleshy, mt_fleshy with untitled2 mat image, dm_maquette, and Ice and Fire (all available through the material library on ZBrush central except for mt_fleshy and mt_fleshy with untitled 2, which came from Diamants Uncharted 2 Artwork thread on the ZBrush Central forums at www.zbrushcentral.com/ showthread.php?t=79141&highlight=uncharted). I've chosen each material for the uniqueness it gives the sculpt as well as the lighting aspects. See Figure 6.9.

2. Through trial and error, I stack the BPR Renders as layers in Photoshop, keeping mt_fleshy at the bottom because it contains the most overall color info. I place each additional MatCap ZBrush image in a new layer on top, alternating different blending modes and Opacity, until I find the perfect combination. See Figure 6.10.

3. Instead of blending the render outputs for each MatCap image, I set the BPR AO (ambient occlusion), Shadow, and Depth to multiply and place them only once at the top of the final stack; this prevents the full composition from being too dark and losing color info. See Figure 6.11.

4. To give a bit more pop and color to the overall composition, I add two more copies of BPR AO: one at the top, set to Overlay and 25% opacity (see Figure 6.12), and a second near the bottom of the stack between the two, mt_Fleshy MatCap. See Figure 6.13.

Figure 6.9 Render settings.

Figure 6.10   MatCaps to be combined.

Figure 6.11   Layered and blended.

Figure 6.12   Layer settings 1.

Figure 6.13   Layer settings 2.

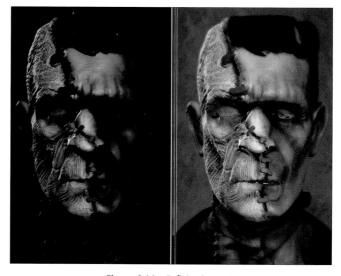

Figure 6.14   Refining image 1.

5. The result gives me quite a nice final image, with a good range of color and flesh tone. Now I just want to add that extra bit of pop and wow to create a really standout image. To start with, I take two merged copies of all the layers and apply the Dark Strokes filter. Then I set the Layer to Multiply and Opacity to 89%. On the second copy, I add a fake depth of field by blurring out the areas around the face, to keep it in focus. I set Layer to Luminosity and Opacity to 44%. See Figure 6.14.

6. Combining them gives me a fairly vibrant and striking image. See Figure 6.15.

7. In the last step, I take a new merged copy of the layers and adjust the levels, contrast, and color balance until I arrive at my final image, shown in Figure 6.16.

TIP

This particular process can tend to go on forever, so be prepared to be a harsh self-critic and know when to call it complete.

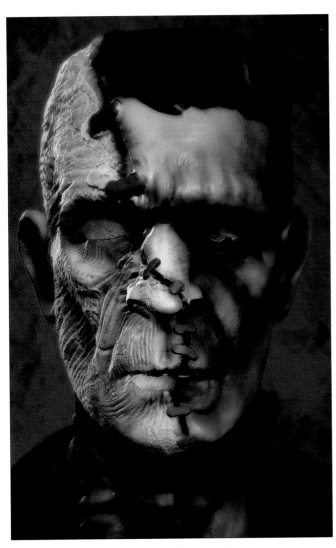

Figure 6.15 Refining image 2.

Figure 6.16 Final image.

KRISTIAN E DAVIDSON

Insights

Q&A

What motivates you or your work?

When I was younger, I had a TV next to my computer and I would work with a movie playing beside me, maybe *Pirates of the Caribbean*, *Lord of the Rings*, or some other big Hollywood FX spectacle. While they very much got the creative juices going, they also had me stopping every few minutes to watch some cool scene or another. These days I try to keep it a bit simpler—a good film score definitely gets me going. I like classical music, but there's something about a soundtrack that moves along to a story and makes it really easy to work to. I usually listen to Hans Zimmer (*Batman* and *Gladiator* in particular), but John Powell Hancock has some really nice pieces; I also like the *Tropic Thunder* score. I keep a decent collection of reference books around me, from game and movie art books to a few stacks of comics. These not only serve as inspiration, but often help solve a particular design problem or just pass some time. They were meant to be read, after all.

Who/what are your inspirations and influences?

I think this is probably typical of many digital artists these days, but *Star Wars* definitely had the biggest influence on me growing up as far as developing an interest in the fantastic. I tend to draw a lot from the so-called "big Hollywood blockbusters" right in the theater where the screen is so big you can just turn off and get lost in the worlds they've created. As a practical artist, though, my biggest inspirations are other game artists. I spend *a lot* of time at www.polycount.com, where there's a strong mix of professionals and students/hobbyists alike. There's an incredible amount of truly awesome art being presented there for display and critique every day.

Which artists do you admire? Why?

There's a ridiculous number of people on that list just in this book alone. When it comes to real-time work, people like Tim Applebee (http://badpolygon.com) and Tom Parker (http://tomparkersartdump.wordpress.com) just blow me away with the style they bring to their craft; and Jon Troy Nickel (www.kalescentstudios.com/troyfolio/Main.htm) makes the sexiest 3D women I've ever seen. For illustration (comics), Jim Lee (www.myspace.com/jimlee00) and Mike Mignola (www.artofmikemignola.com/) couldn't be further apart, but they both are able to convey such tremendous energy in a still image that each new panel is a visual treat.

When did you start using ZBrush?

I started using ZBrush a little over two years ago while working on an entry for an online character competition. I had used *that other sculpting program* the previous year, but after seeing what ZBrush could do with ZSpheres and Polygroups alone, I just had to try it for myself.

Describe your creative process and workflow. How does ZBrush fit?

More and more ZBrush is taking over my workflow. Typically, I start with a doodle of some kind, fairly light and more about the idea than anything too specific (unless for a client or contest), and then I either use ZSpheres directly to further explore the concept or build a base mesh in Maya to set up the proportions and various accessories. From there I import the various parts into ZBrush and create the high-poly sculpt, which I then turn around and bring back into Maya to create the low-poly, real-time version. It's a bit of back and forth, but with features like GoZ, it's a wonderfully simple process.

What's your workflow? Do you create from scratch with ZSpheres, or do you import geometry from another package to work on or develop?

As I get more comfortable in ZBrush, I'm starting to spend much more time in it and less with external programs unless absolutely necessary. With my last few pieces, I've started by creating a ZSpheres Base mesh, used GoZ to bring it into Maya for a quick retop, and then gone back to ZBrush where I can finish up the sculpt without worrying too much about density/detail issues that can occur with straight ZSpheres bases.

What are some of your favorite ZBrush features? How do you use them?

Most of my favorites are just the basic sculpting tools—the Clay Tubes and dmStandard in particular. I do love using the Planks Brush for certain types of skin detail—lizard stuff in particular. With the right tweaks and pen pressure, it's a surprisingly versatile brush, and it's actually what I used to create most of the rotting bandages in my "Karloff the Uncanny" piece (in the later section "Gallery," titled "Frank Final").

How are you using TimeLine?

I have yet to really explore TimeLine, but I have a few ideas involving layer transitions that should really change the way I can present a model.

Are you using SpotLight to texture or for sculptural details? Please explain.

So far, I've been using SpotLight exclusively for projection painting texture details onto Polypainted characters. For the "Vampire Frogmen of Neptune," for example, after laying down some base colors, I painted over the top with a few different skin and rock textures from my personal library at a low Opacity setting. Blending them directly on the model, I was able to get a final skin texture that I wouldn't have found with Polypaint or Photoshop alone.

Are you using ShadowBox to make base meshes? How?

I built Heavy Henry's Gatling gun (see "Henry Final" and "Henry Final Turns" in the later section titled "Gallery") using ShadowBox for the more uncommon shapes, like the top handle and the firing crank. Along with some default cylinders for barrels and drums, I was able to use ShadowBox to make the whole gun in just a few hours.

Are you using any of the new brushes in ZBrush, like the Move Elastic Brush?

Move Elastic is a great tool for random pointy bits like hair detail or bat wings on a monkey.

What are you using for hard edge modeling?

Hard edge modeling in ZBrush is tricky. I've tried a few experiments so far with the Trim Brushes and the Flatten/Polish Brushes with different levels of success, but my comfort with Maya has kept me from really going all out. Other ZBrush artists pull it off, though, so it's just a matter of time before I dive right in.

Are you using ZSketch? How?

I love using ZSketch for hair! Being able to place it on my character and style it before I even get into the sculpting is a lot of fun and creates some pretty unique images I couldn't get with just a base mesh.

What tools do you most often use to texture? SpotLight? Image Plane? Projection Master? ZAppLink?

On my current projects, I use a mix of Polypainting and SpotLight with Photoshop for cleanup or specific needs.

How do you use BPR for rendering out your final image?

Aside from some slight adjustments to the Shadow and AO settings, I don't mess with the default BPR too much. I've started using a little Depth of Field, and I added some Fog to Karloff, but for the most part the defaults have given me what I need.

Are you using Photoshop overlay for your final image?

In the past, I've used Photoshop to compile the images outputted from BPR, but usually only when I intended to change the background and did not want to alias the image with a selection mask that didn't already have an alpha channel. For the pieces featured in Technique 2, I've made extensive use of Photoshop, trying out different layering and blending techniques to get the best possible picture I can and creating more illustrative pieces than simple character renders.

ZBrush lighting is much more complex than ever before. Do you use any of the advanced features? Which ones? Material generating?

I get most of my lighting info from combining different MatCaps and using BPR to bring out the extra shadow/AO detail.

Which ZPlugs do you use? How?

I'm definitely a fan of SubTool Master for organizing my scenes and Transpose Master for posing multiple SubTools. Decimation Master is indispensable for real-time (game) art.

What are your favorite new sculpting tools?

I really like the possibilities the new Deco Brushes offer for detailing. I can get some unique and interesting details with the defaults or just quickly swapping out the alpha and adjusting the Focal Shift.

How do you use customizable tools in ZBrush?

Being able to adjust how the tools respond as I go is about as helpful as it can get. Things like the automasking settings, where I can turn BackfaceMask on and off for different brushes to prevent clipping (or clean it up) has been a lifesaver. I just remember that it needs to be off for the Move tools to work properly.

What are some of your time-saving tips when using ZBrush on a work project or for personal artwork?

Using the Projects function is probably the biggest time saver I've come across. Not needing to reset things like the active material and BPR setup can save a good five minutes that I can then spend actually working.

What advice do you have for artists working with ZBrush?

When working on a sculpt, it's best to start at the lowest resolution possible and only move to the next level when nothing else can be added. I see the opposite constantly with new artists and have been told about it a few dozen times myself. Starting at the bottom allows building of the underlying structure of the sculpt, giving it a real sense of weight that is a lot harder to capture at the 2 million poly mark.

What do you wish someone had told you when you started with ZBrush?

I wish someone had told me I should spend some real time learning to use the program. Just jumping in and expecting highly detailed, lifelike sculpts usually leads to disappointment.

How has ZBrush helped you successfully define your own graphic/artistic style?

I've developed a fairly loose sketching style over the years, inspired by a mix of classic animation from Disney and Warner Bros in the 1950s to a few more modern comic artists. With ZBrush, I've been able to translate that into the 3D realm fairly quickly, creating a tighter, more unified look.

Resources

Links

- www.polycount.com
- www.zbrushcentral.com
- www.gameartisans.org
- www.cgtalk.com

KRISTIAN E DAVIDSON

Contact

Kristian E Davidson ■ Rabbit Hole Interactive ■ Richmond BC, Canada, V7C 4K5 ■ kedavidson@shaw.ca ■ kedavidson.blogspot.com

Education/Experience

Graduated with a degree in animation design ■ Freelance character artist ■ 3D artist at Tribbo Post and Techno Image

Awards and Career Highlights

Certificates in game art and design from AI Vancouver and Vancouver Film School (VFS)

Hardware/Software Used with ZBrush

Hardware: At home a dual-core processor, 4GB of RAM; At work 6GB RAM, dual-monitor

Software: Maya, TopoGun

KRISTIAN E DAVIDSON

Gallery

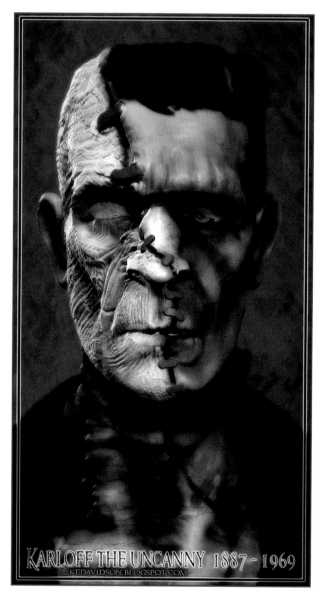

"Frank Final."

"Prince Final001."

KRISTIAN E DAVIDSON

KRISTIAN E DAVIDSON

"Prince Final003."

Prince not—so Charming
KEDAVIDSON.BLOGSPOT.COM

"Prince Final004."

KRISTIAN E DAVIDSON

HEAVY HENRY
KEDAVIDSON.BLOGSPOT.COM

"Henry Final Turns."

"Henry Final."

"Monkey Portrait."

"Monkey Pose."

BRIAN HABERLIN

About the Artist

I am an award-winning comic book creator, writer, illustrator, fine artist, and educator. I cocreated the popular *Witchblade* comic, which was also a television show. I also created numerous other comic titles from *Captain Wonder* to *Hellcop*, which is currently in development for a feature film. I am finishing a 375-page graphic novel titled *Anomaly*. Besides owning and creating tutorials for www.digitalarttutorials.com, I am a teacher of comic art at Minneapolis College of Art and Design and a contributor to *3D World* and *ImagineFX* magazine. My work is in the permanent collection at the Smithsonian Museum.

Artist's Statement

I take sort of a Faustian approach to art—in other words, any means to an end. The end, of course, is hopefully a version of what is in my head brought out to the real world. I smash together analogue, digital, oil, 3D, coffee, dirt—you name it—to get the image right.

Second page from graphic novel *Anomaly*.

Techniques

Technique 1:
How to Make a Fully Textured Mesh in No Time

Okay, here is how to make a fully textured mesh. This technique can be used for anything from details on costumes to full-blown sets (see Figure 7.1).

1. I start with the image I want to have created as a 3D mesh.

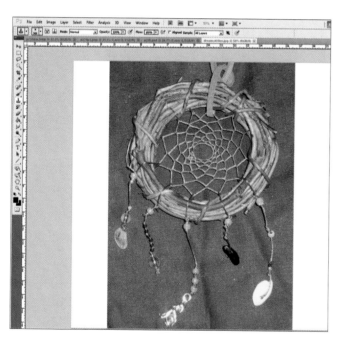

Figure 7.1   Choose an image that will become a 3D mesh.

2. I chose this image because it would probably take a few hours to create a model of it using conventional methods—and more time to texture it. I begin in Photoshop with the image. I isolate what I want to make into the mesh, as if I'm making a silhouette of the shape, using a selection tool. Once the dream catcher is selected, I copy it to another layer (see Figure 7.2).

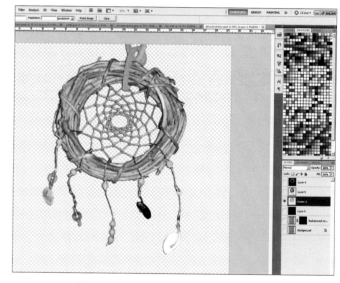

Figure 7.2   Isolate the image with Photoshop.

3. I load that new layer as a selection (by holding the Ctrl/Cmd key on that layer in the Layer menu) and make a new layer above the copied layer. I fill the silhouette selection of the dream catcher with black and begin to rough in its shape with a soft white brush. What I am making here is a rough "height map" of the dream catcher.

This does not need to be too detailed, because my texture map will drive most of the detail on this model anyway. I just want the general shape here. I drop the opacity of this layer to about 60% so I can see the detail of the original image below. I save this out as a JPG and name it (see Figure 7.3).

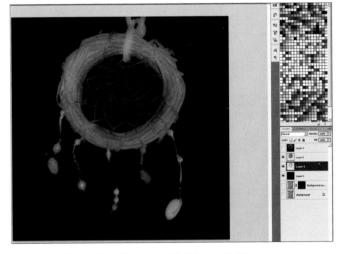

Figure 7.3   Make a rough "height map" of the image.

Figure 7.4   Move the image to ZBrush and load Plane 3D.

NOTE

Giving the image UV coordinates is not necessary in ZBrush 3.5, but it is in ZBrush 4.

4. Moving to ZBrush, I start by loading Plane 3D. I make sure I am in Edit mode and then convert the image to a polymesh by using the Make PolyMesh3d button. Next, I use the ZPlugin UV Master to give the image UV coordinates. Then I subdivide the polymeshed Plane 3D. High res is necessary here to drive the detail in the mesh I will be creating; I go to about 4 million polys (see Figure 7.4).

5. I load the JPG I made of the "height map" version of the dream catcher as an alpha. Now in the Masking menu, I choose Mask by Alpha. The alpha appears on the plane. I go to Deformation, turn the plane a bit so I can see the effect, and increase the Inflat setting. My dream catcher shape pokes out of the plane (see Figure 7.5).

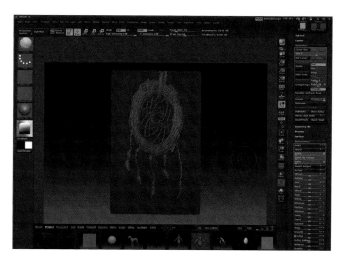

Figure 7.5 Choose Mask by Alpha.

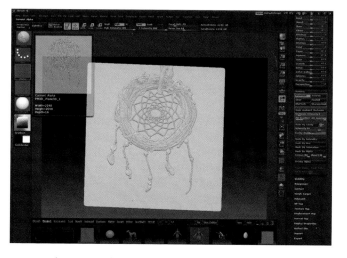

Figure 7.6 Choose Mask by Cavity and then Create Alpha.

6. I clear the mask and create a new one, but first I make my UV map 4096 so I have high detail to work from. I choose Mask by Cavity and then Create Alpha (see Figure 7.6).

7. I export that alpha. In Photoshop, it's easy to select all the areas where the mesh isn't and fill them with black, and fill the areas where the mesh is with white (see Figure 7.7).

8. I save and load this image into ZBrush as a new alpha. In the Masking menu, I use Mask by Alpha, Inverse. Next, in the Visibility menu, I select HidePt. I'm left with just my dream catcher (see Figure 7.8). It's one sided, so I'm going to fix it.

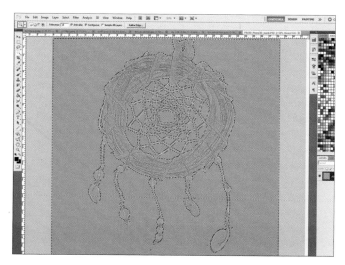

Figure 7.7 Export the alpha and in Photoshop fill selected areas.

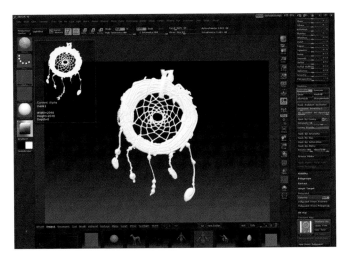

Figure 7.8　One-sided image.

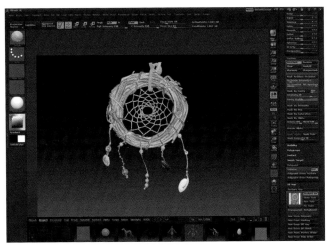

Figure 7.9　Delete the geometry and import the original color texture.

9. I need to delete the geometry I have hidden. Under the Geometry menu, use Del Lower and then Del Hidden to get rid of the hidden mesh. In that same panel, I use Mirror and Weld set to Z only. My dream catcher now has a backside. Next, I import the original color texture, go to the Texture Map menu, and turn Texture On (see Figure 7.9).

10. I select my imported map, and bingo bongo I have a fully textured model in a matter of minutes. I clean up any jagged geometry using Deformation/Polish. I recommend loading the original color file in SpotLight to clean up any textures (see Figure 7.10).

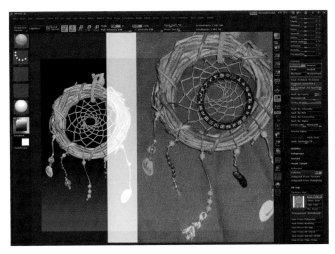

Figure 7.10　Select the imported map. You now have a fully textured model!

TIP

To really apply textures with more control, use SpotLight.

Insights

Q&A

What motivates you or your work?

Getting the ideas out of my brain motivates me, as does the pure joy of creation.

Who/what are your inspirations and influences?

Anyone who is good, is innovative, and can consistently produce fine work or continue to improve previous work inspires me.

Which artists do you admire? Why?

There are so many I admire, but off the top of my head, I admire Miyazaki and Tim Burton for their imagination; Jean Giraud (Mobius) for everything; Wayne Barlowe for his pencil work; J.C. Leyendecker for pretty images; and Rockwell Kent for bold images. The list could go on and on.

When did you start using ZBrush?

I started using it when it first came out, but not really majorly until version 3.

Describe your creative process and workflow. How does ZBrush fit?

ZBrush has a role in almost every 3D model I either create or customize, from pure scratch models done entirely in the program to new textures and morph targets for customizing existing ones.

What's your workflow? Do you create from scratch with ZSpheres or import geometry from another package to work on/develop?

Really I do both; it just depends on what I need to make. ShadowBox is now part of those tools as well.

What are some of your favorite ZBrush features? How do you use them?

I use SpotLight, UV Master, and Decimation Master *a lot*—especially when I'm making props. I sculpt these really heavy geometry pieces that look great but would be impossible to use in other software. That's where Decimation Master comes in; it brings the pieces down to feather weight, and they still look great!

Are you using SpotLight to texture or for sculptural details?

I mostly use SpotLight for texture but often use that texture as a mask to pull out some of the fine details. If I use pictures/ textures for modeling reference, my silhouette is pretty much there already, and the texture and a little detail bump from the texture are usually all I need.

Are you using ShadowBox to make base meshes? How?

I use it mostly for bits and bobs, like vents and knobs on tech armor, or buckles and rivets in low-tech armor.

Are you using any of the new brushes in ZBrush, like the Move Elastic Brush?

I use move Topological a lot when customizing existing figures. I can move individual teeth in a mesh without having to separate them as ZTools or with masking—a real time saver.

What are you using for hard edge modeling?

I'm using a good deal of custom brushes, including the Planar, Polish, and Damien Standard Brush. Also, I like to paint groups and limit the brush tolerance accordingly.

Are you using ZSketch? How?

I don't use it that much. I usually model in other programs, at least for a base mesh.

What tools do you most often use to texture? SpotLight? Image Plane? Projection Master? ZAppLink?

I usually use SpotLight and Image Plane. For head modeling ref, I usually use Image Plane to get a quick likeness.

How do you use Best Preview Render (BPR) for rendering out your final image?

I usually export my ZBrush models to other applications for rendering.

How do you use customizable tools in ZBrush?

I often grab detail from another piece of geometry and create an alpha from that already sculpted geometry using GrabDoc in the alpha menu. This is great for adding all kinds of detail quickly.

ZBrush has so many tools that it's easy to get lost. I focus on the ones that fit my workflow. Not feeling like I have to use them all speeds up my work!

What advice do you have for artists working with ZBrush?

My advice is to grab some real clay. Sculpting in the real world helps your ZBrush work, and it's fun to get your hands dirty.

What do you wish someone had told you when you started with ZBrush?

I wish someone had told me that the learning curve was worth it!

How has ZBrush helped you successfully define your own graphic/artistic style?

It's given me the tools to more accurately reproduce what I see in my head.

Resources

Links

- www.Goodbrush.com
- www.Zbrushcentral.com
- www.instructables.com
- www.linesandcolors.com
- www.digitalarttutorials.com

BRIAN HABERLIN

Contact

Brian Haberlin ■ Laguna Niguel, CA 92677 ■ bhaberlin@digitalarttutorials.com ■ www.digitalarttutorials.com

Education/Experience

Professional artist since a teen ■ Master's degree in communication arts

Awards and Career Highlights

Wizard Fan awards, Eagle awards, Eisner awards

Client List

DreamWorks, Disney, Marvel Comics, DC Comics, Verizon, NASCAR, *TV Guide*, TopCow Productions, Universal Studios, Warner Bros., *Spin Magazine*, Bandai, Pacific Data Images, Stan Winston Creatures, Sammy Studios, and many more

Hardware/Software Used with ZBrush

Hardware: I always try to use the fastest processor available with the most RAM.

Software: Photoshop, Poser Pro, 3ds Max, Maya

BRIAN HABERLIN

Gallery

A spread from the *Anomaly* graphic novel. Texture and creature morphs done in ZBrush.

BRIAN HABERLIN

From *Anomaly* graphic novel. Some texture, prop, morph on each character is done in ZBrush.

BRIAN HABERLIN

Page from *Anomaly* graphic novel. Terrain, morphs, and texturing done in ZBrush.

Examples of characters customized in ZBrush for use in Poser.

Page from *Anomaly* graphic novel. Fish beast detailed and morph created in ZBrush.

Spread from *Shifter* graphic novel. Textures and morphs from ZBrush.

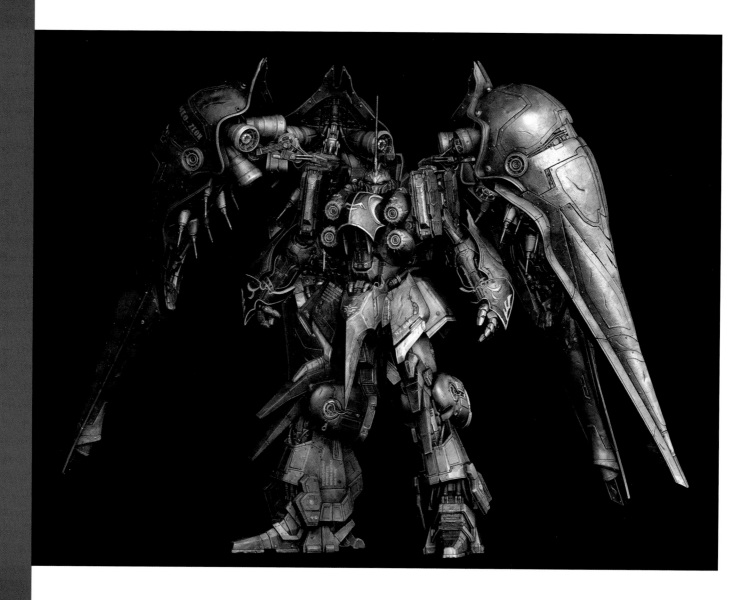

IOANNIS KARATHOMAS

IOANNIS KARATHOMAS

About the Artist

I have always liked to draw. As a kid, I copied Disney characters and comic book heroes. I grew up thinking of ways to redesign some of my favorite heroes because of my love for manga, anime, and comic books.

Though I was born in Greece, I studied at the Gnomon School of Visual Arts in Los Angeles. I decided to make my hobby a career, and I've never regretted it because I can't think of anything else that I would rather do for a living.

Every artist has strong skills; mine are in hard surface modeling. I'm trying to get better at sculpting crazy, organic creatures and cute, stylized characters.

Artist's Statement

Some people say that art is a form of self-expression. I like to make art that is beautiful, stunning, and simple to understand.

As an artist, I challenge myself; it's how I move forward and become better.

"NZ 666 Kshatria."

Techniques

Technique 1: Production Workflow

From my years of experience, I've come to understand the importance of traditional sculpting and a base model block in 3D software. ZBrush is fast and powerful software that can create a faster workflow.

In this technique, I show you the basic steps of how you can create a character from ZSpheres, texture it, and retopologize it for game production.

1. By selecting a ZSphere, I can create a base armature for my character more quickly than blocking a base mesh in other 3D software. After I select a ZSphere by pressing Shift+A, I switch to Sketch mode. Sketch mode allows me to draw and manipulate a series of spheres to build a fast blockout for my character.

TIP

Keep in mind that while you sketch in Sketch mode, you combine multiple ZSpheres. Therefore, the more you add, the heavier your polycount is. You can control that by pressing Shift to smooth your mesh and Alt to delete spheres.

2. I can view my mesh by pressing A. Sometimes when I have a complicated ZSketch and I try to view my mesh, the geometry does not look the way it is supposed to. In that case, I navigate to the Tool menu under Unified Skin Subpalette, where I can turn up the resolution and smoothing until I am happy with my mesh. The higher the resolution, the heavier the mesh. See Figure 8.1.

Figure 8.1 ZSketch blockout.

3. When I finish the ZSketch, I press A. On the Tool panel, I click Make Polymesh3D, which creates a new file with my mesh that is not a ZSphere and allows me to sculpt it freely. If I decide later on that I want to add geometry like horns, I can add a new ZSphere and draw the shape. I create a new Polymesh 3D, append it, bake it to my mesh, and merge the SubTools. That allows me to sculpt the shapes as if there were one from the beginning. See Figure 8.2.

Figure 8.2 ZSketch sculptable mesh.

4. When I finish, I have a base mesh that allows me to start blocking my character.

TIP

Know your goal and use a lot of references; they can save you time and trouble from guessing.

5. With the Clay Tubes Brush, I create my silhouette and shape all the big forms and muscles. Clay Tubes provides a nice texture on the mesh. After I finish blocking out my shape, I start working on the details and define the muscle groups. It's easy to lose the details. See Figure 8.3.

Figure 8.3 Defined muscles and form.

6. To separate the muscle groups, I use the Standard Brush because it enables me to draw basic straight lines and create depth and cuts on my mesh easier than the other brushes. Then I use the Clay Tubes Brush to blend overlaying muscles, like the ones on the neck of my character. See Figure 8.4.

IOANNIS KARATHOMAS

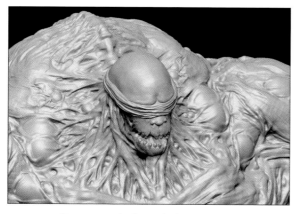

Figure 8.4 Blending with Clay Tubes Brush.

7. After I blend overlaying muscles, I start working on all the extra details in my creature, like scratches, veins, and wrinkles. See Figures 8.5, 8.6, and 8.7.

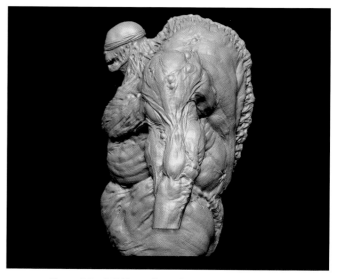

Figure 8.6 Wrinkles and scratches with Clay Tubes Brush.

Figure 8.5 Veins with Clay Tubes Brush.

Figure 8.7 Defined spine with Clay Tubes Brush.

8. Texturing a creature's flesh is a challenge because it's hard to find textures. Hand texturing is often required. To begin texturing, I select a white skin shader, go to the Polypaint menu, and turn on Colorize. On the top bar menu, I click on the color I want with low Opacity and click Fill Object. That gives me a flat base color to start working. When you Polypaint and use the Spray Brush with alpha, ZBrush gives you two varieties of colors: the color you chose and a slightly darker version of that color. Under the stroke menu on the left are the Color Intensity Variance and Flow Variance controllers, where you can adjust the values.

9. I like to use a Standard Brush with the 07 alpha and a spray stroke that gives me a variety of color while I paint; that way, it will look like small pores on the skin. I make sure on the Stroke menu that I turn Color Intensity Variance off; otherwise, I have two different colors while I paint. Sometimes I do like that variety if I keep the Opacity setting low. Under the stroke menu on the left, you can find the Color Intensity Variance and the Flow Variance controllers where you can adjust the values.

10. I want to start blocking out my skin color by painting the subdermal. I paint light yellow colors wherever there are bones, dark red on the muscles, and dark blue or purple on the deep negative spaces between the muscles to arrive at a deep skin color variation. See Figure 8.8.

11. When I finish, I select the DragRect stoke with the alpha 22 with red or blue to draw some veins. The last thing I need to do is draw soft colors with the spray brush to create epidermal skin that looks more natural. See Figure 8.9.

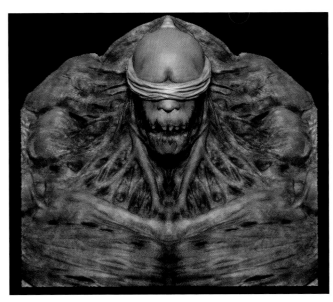

Figure 8.8 Skin color for realism.

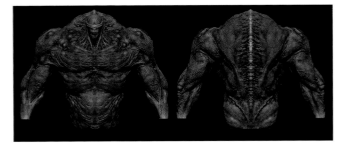

Figure 8.9 Natural skin color using DragRect.

IOANNIS KARATHOMAS

12. I use the Higher Res button located in Tool, Geometry, select a ZSphere, and in the Tool menu open the Adaptive Skin subpalette, Rigging subpalette, and Topology menu. I might hide the rest. On the Rigging subpalette, I click and select Mesh, select my high-res sculpture, and place the ZSphere on the center of the mesh. On the Topology subpalette, I click Edit Topology so I can start resurfacing my mesh. Symmetry can be activated if needed. By clicking Ctrl, I can place dots on my mesh and start connecting the vertices to build the new mesh.

13. Pressing the A button allows me to preview my mesh. If I can't see detail, I can increase the density on the Adaptive Skin subpalette. When I finish, I can project my extra details if I need to. See Figure 8.10.

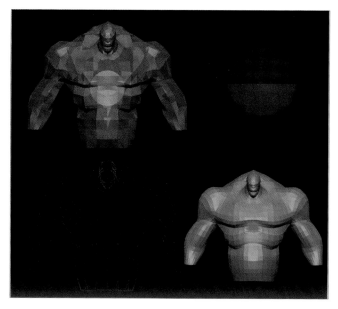

Figure 8.10 Retopology and reprojecting.

14. In the final step, I append the new mesh and subdivide it. In the Tool menu, the SubTool subpalette has a ProjectAll button. I can click that and reproject all the high-res details and color paint to my new mesh. See Figure 8.11.

Figure 8.11 Finalizing the mesh.

15. In my production workflow, I usually export the lowest subdivision object and load that object either to Headus UV Layout or into Maya to place my UVs. Sometimes I texture my high-res images in ZBrush and create a new retopologized mesh. I use the ZBrush PUV Tiles to create automatic UVs and bake my Polypaint into a new texture in ZBrush. Then I export my high-res mesh and my texture map and load them into Maya. See Figures 8.12, 8.13, and 8.14.

IOANNIS KARATHOMAS

Figure 8.12   Front view completed texturing.

Figure 8.13   Back view completed texturing.

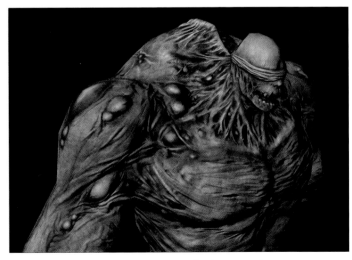

Figure 8.14   ¾ turn completed texturing view.

IOANNIS KARATHOMAS

Insights

Q&A

What motivates you or your work?

I want to become a better artist, so I study the art of the masters to inspire and teach me.

Who/what are your inspirations and influences?

Despite my years in the industry, I still consider myself to be a young artist. I'm always eager to learn more so that I can become a better artist. The past few years, I was privileged enough to work on commercial short films and games. I'm always looking for a challenge. Whenever I create a personal project, I try to do something difficult to increase my skills and my knowledge.

I grew up playing video games and reading comics; as a result, my inspirations and influences came from my favorite artists such as Gerald Brom, Frank Frazetta, and Michael Turner. I also admire concept artists like Keith Thompson, Paul Richard, and Wei Wang. Those artists have unique talents, and they inspire me in different ways to become a better artist. I will always admire the work of the masters, and I will continue working hard to reach their level.

What are some of your favorite ZBrush features? How do you use them?

In ZBrush, all the tools are great, but one of my favorite ZBrush features is the Decimation Master plug-in. I usually end up working with subdivisions in my mesh, so before Decimation Master, I had large file problems with exporting to a high-res mesh. I use the Decimation Master to lower the polygons on my mesh, but only after I have completed my sculpture. I make sure I have a backup because it changes the topology of my mesh and prohibits me from sculpting on it anymore.

Another favorite feature is ZSketch, which allows me to block out a character in just a few minutes, saving me a lot of time. I have to retopologize to use my sculpt on other software. I use the Best Preview Render (BPR) to render high-quality passes in ZBrush and composite them in Photoshop. I also love the GoZ, of course. It allows me to send my mesh back and forth from ZBrush to Maya (or other 3D modeling software) and change the topology.

What advice do you have for artists working with ZBrush?

ZBrush is powerful software, but it is the artist who utilizes the software's strength. There are so many amazing artists out there that the industry is frightening at the same time it is inspiring. I recommend forgetting about topology, because a mesh can always be resurfaced later. I always look at my reference.

What do you wish someone had told you when you started with ZBrush?

My advice for a beginner is that when creating a character, the first focus should be on creating a dynamic pose and gesture and to making sure proportions are appropriate.

When did you start using ZBrush?

I was introduced to ZBrush 2.0 about five years ago when I was still a student. Since then, Pixologic team has answered the industry demands and created software that is fast, efficient, and makes productivity faster than any other software.

Describe your creative process and workflow. How does ZBrush fit?

My process always depends on my goal. I used to build a base mesh in Maya and import the object into ZBrush, sculpt all the details, bake normal maps and textures, and then render my sculpt in Maya. Now I often start with ZSphere blocking and then resurface my mesh.

Are you using SpotLight for texture or for sculptural details? Please explain.

I always sculpt with a standard gray material. Rotating the SpotLight helps me see how deep or high my details are from the surface. It's also helpful when I want to create clean and round surfaces, like female faces or cartoon characters

What are you using for hard edge modeling?

For hard surface sculpting, I prefer to use the Polish Brushes to define the shape of my mesh. I start sculpting scratches on the surface and with the Standard Brush. After that, I get the Pinch Brush and start pinching the edges. As soon as I finish, I select a Polish Brush and start damaging the surface and the edges to look like beat metal. Finally, I use alphas to draw bolts and surface details. I save a morph target in every step, just in case I want to switch to my previous version.

What tools do you most often use to texture? SpotLight? Image Plane? Projection Master? ZAppLink?

For texturing, I prefer to use Polypaint, but when it comes to doing something realistic like a human face, I use ZAppLink to project texture to make my mesh 3D.

Are you using Photoshop overlay for your final image? Describe.

Unless I want to render a turn table, it is nice to render different passes in ZBrush and compose them in Photoshop to achieve my goal. I usually render a diffuse pass and occlusion pass and a shadow and a spec pass.

Which ZPlugs do you use? How?

I use the Decimation Master when my mesh gets heavy and I want to export my high-res object. I also use the Multi Map Exporter to bake multiple textures quickly. My favorite tool is GoZ because it helps me to transfer my mesh from ZBrush to Maya with a click of a button without having to export or import objects.

What are your favorite new sculpting tools?

I really enjoy the Planar Brush because it helps define hard surface silhouettes. Also, the Clipping Brush is nice if I want to cut my mesh.

IOANNIS KARATHOMAS

Contact
Ioannis@jkarathomas.com ▪ www.jkarathomas.com

Education/Experience
Gnomon School of Visual Effects ▪ California Akto Art and Design ▪ Middlesex University of London

Hardware/Software Used with ZBrush
Hardware: Intel Core 7 with 6GB RAM and Nvidia GeForce GTX 460; Windows 7 64-bit machine

Software: Maya, 3ds Max, Mudbox, Photoshop, Renderman, Unreal Engine, Flash, After Effects

IOANNIS KARATHOMAS

IOANNIS KARATHOMAS

Gallery

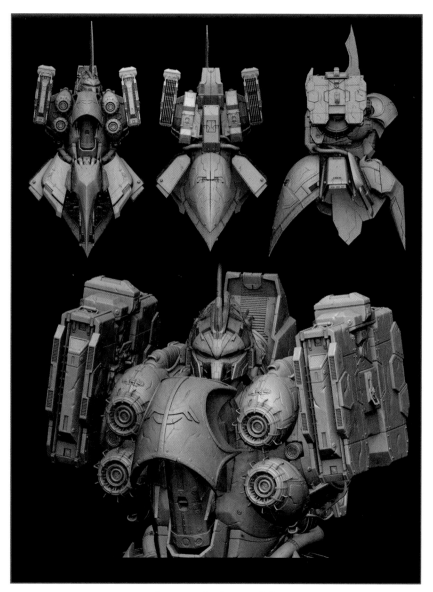

"NZ_666_Kshatria01 Details."

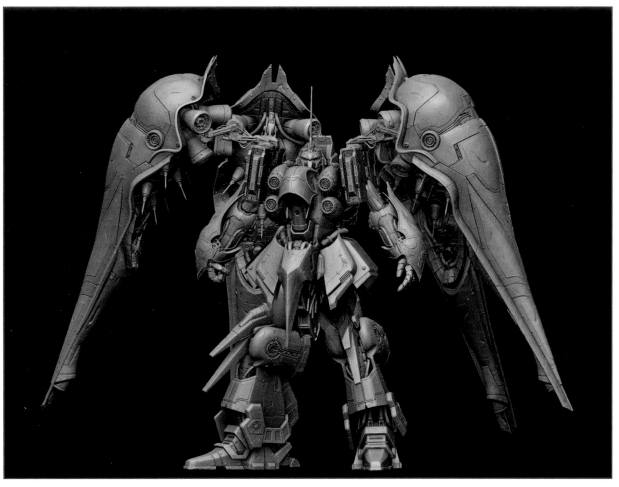

"NZ_666_Kshatria Beauty."

IOANNIS KARATHOMAS

"Soulfire Grace Body."

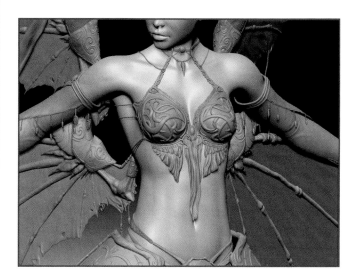

"Soulfire Grace Close-Up."

"Soulfire Grace."

IOANNIS KARATHOMAS

"Demon 1."

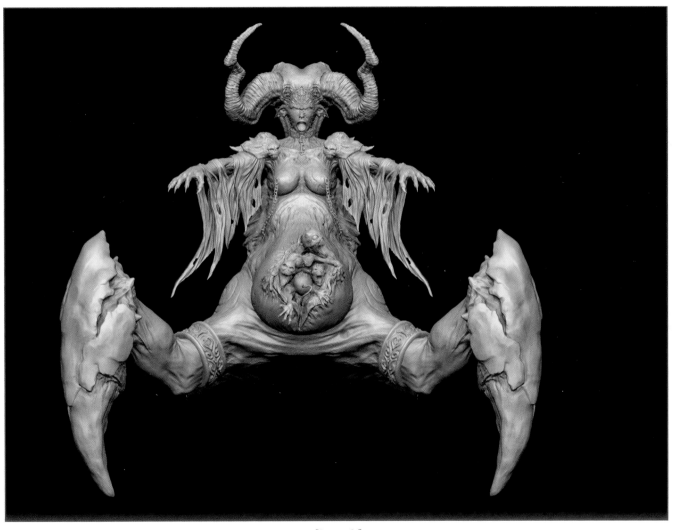

"Demon 2."

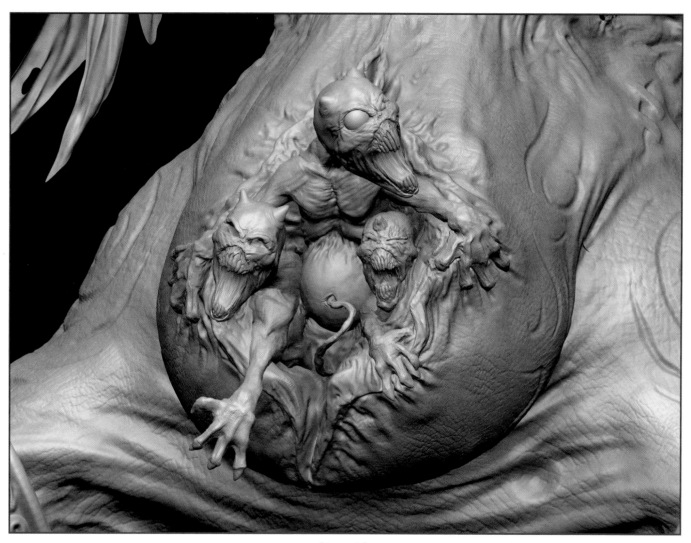

"Demon 3."

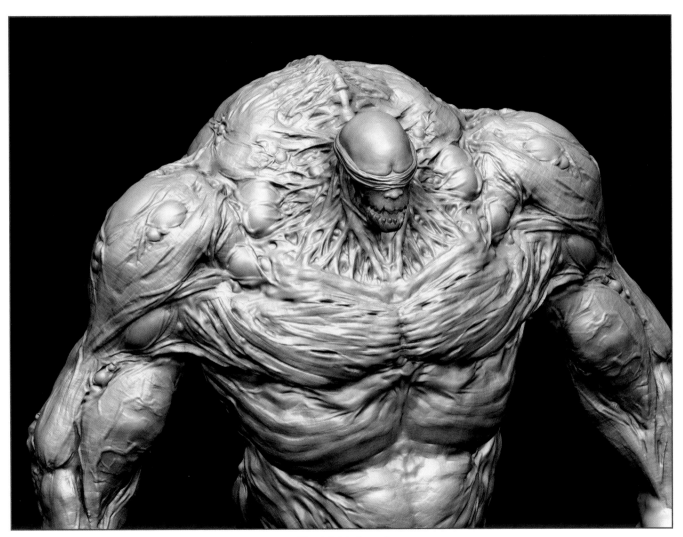

"Death Knight Beauty."

IOANNIS KARATHOMAS

"Death Knight Orthographic."

"Death Knight Close."

ANDRZEJ KUZIOLA

About the Artist

I am a self-taught artist now working as a freelance illustrator and 3D artist. I specialize mainly in character creation and really enjoy it. Beside illustration and 3D jobs, I write training articles for *3D Artist Magazine*. ZBrush, Cinema 4D, and Photoshop help me create realms existing only in my mind.

Artist's Statement

Having the ability to create something that exists only in your mind is unbelievable. I find it interesting when there is more than one way of seeing things and when illustrations are more complex, which allows most of my illustrations to be open to interpretation.

"Sound of the Sea."

ANDRZEJ KUZIOLA

Techniques

Technique 1: Creating and Detailing Geometry

In my first tutorial, I show how to use ZSpheres and Sculpting Brushes to create interesting geometry—a vertebra—which I am going to use to build more complex geometry.

1. I select a ZSphere from the Tool palette and draw it on the canvas.

2. I press X on my keyboard to activate symmetry mode and reduce Brush Draw Size to 1. This allows me to select just one ZSphere at a time without affecting neighbor areas. I start to draw more ZSpheres on the surface of the first one, trying to match ZSphere's rig to the shape of a reference vertebra image in an anatomy atlas. I use Q, W, and E shortcuts to switch between Draw, Move, and Scale mode, attempting to make the armature look like the reference (see Figure 9.1).

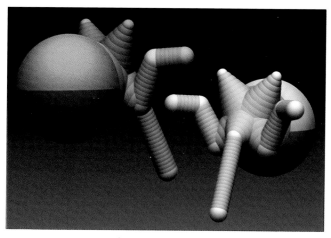

Figure 9.1 ZSpheres rig.

3. By pressing the A key, I can quickly preview how the final mesh will look. When I am happy with the result, I change the rig to Adaptive Skin located in the Tool menu and then press the Make Polymesh3D button to add more details. I do so by choosing the Tool menu, Adaptive Skin subpalette, Make Adaptive Skin. I scroll up and select Make Polymesh3D with the new created skin selected (see Figure 9.2).

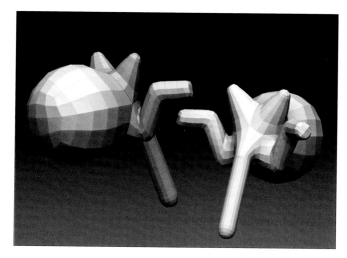

Figure 9.2 Polymesh3D.

4. I modify the shape of the mesh with the Move and Move Elastic Brushes with the help of the Smooth Brush. I work on the low-resolution mesh (see Figure 9.3).

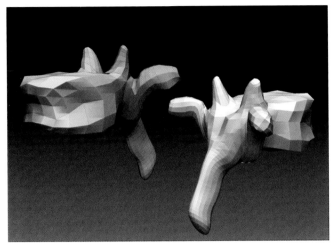

Figure 9.3 Reshaping the mesh.

Figure 9.4 Sculpting.

5. I subdivide the mesh a few times with a Ctrl+D shortcut and start sculpting with the Clay, TrimDynamic, and Smooth Brushes. The mesh looks more and more like the reference (see Figure 9.4).

6. I add more details with the Standard Brush, switching between mesh subdivisions with the D and Shift+D shortcuts during the process. It's best to utilize each subdivision level as much as possible before switching to a higher resolution (see Figure 9.5).

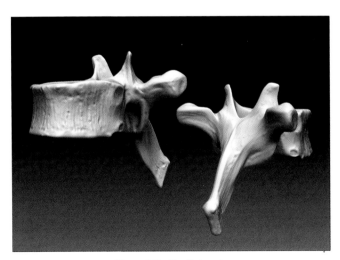

Figure 9.5 Detailed mesh.

ANDRZEJ KUZIOLA

Technique 2: Composting SubTools

In this tutorial, I use the geometry created in the previous tutorial to build a more complex object.

1. I select my Vertebra Polymesh and then select Duplicate in the SubTool palette. I select the newly created tool on the SubTools list and then switch to Move mode by pressing the W shortcut and moving it above the first one. I repeat the process a few times. My goal is to create the spinal column (see Figure 9.6).

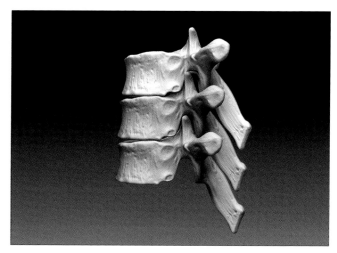

Figure 9.6 Building the spinal column.

2. I use the Move Brush to diversify the shapes of the vertebrae. Then I click the Merge Down button to connect the SubTools and create a new, complex one. I use Move Brush with a large Draw Size to modify the shape of the spinal column (see Figure 9.7).

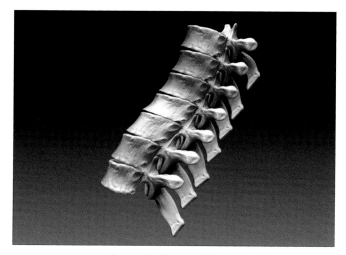

Figure 9.7 Shape modification.

TIP

Be open minded, and don't let anything limit your imagination.

3. With the new geometry selected, I start SubTool Master in the ZPlugin menu and select the Mirror with Merged into One SubTool option (see Figure 9.8).

Figure 9.8   Spinal column mirrored.

Insights

Q&A

Who/what are your inspirations and influences?

Music is my most important inspiration. Sometimes it is just a short phrase from lyrics that triggers the creation process. I start to develop the ideas based on my own interpretation of the fragment. I always listen to music when I create.

I love to trek through the wilderness of Scotland because nature is another inspiration for me. Beautiful colors and breathtaking landscapes influence my art.

I look for ideas in faces of people I pass on a street, in shapes hidden on stained old walls, or in colors of corroded metal.

The entire world around me is inspiration. I just see it in a different way when I close my eyes.

When did you start using ZBrush?

My first contact with ZBrush was about six years ago. It was ZBrush 2. I used it to detail meshes imported from Softimage XSI and to create displacement maps. I started to use ZBrush more and more after the ZBrush 3 release. Now ZBrush 4 is my main 3D tool—from creating initial meshes to rendering.

**Describe your creative process and workflow.
How does ZBrush fit?**

I never sketch out my ideas. When I have the idea in my head, I start straight in 3D and then experiment and develop it in the 3D environment. I use references in a limited way. I don't want to copy reality.

Most of the time I start in ZBrush with ZSpheres. Then when I am happy with the result, I convert it to PolyMesh3D and start sculpting and adding details.

ANDRZEJ KUZIOLA

ZBrush is great for developing ideas. I can explore new shapes and forms in a fast and efficient way without worrying about technical aspects.

I use ZSpheres for organic shapes or import geometry from another package as a base mesh for hard surface objects. When it is more convenient for me to create a particular model in another 3D application, I do so and import it to ZBrush for further detailing. When a model is ready, I retopologize it and create UVs in ZBrush.

Thanks to SpotLight, the texturing process is fast and intuitive. I can paint textures in ZBrush even before establishing UVs.

Depending on the result I want to achieve, I render everything with Best Preview Render (BPR) as separate passes or export a decimated scene to Cinema 4D, where I use Advanced Renderer. I do post-production with Photoshop.

What are some of your favorite ZBrush features? How do you use them?

One of my favorite ZBrush features is ZSpheres. They are a starting point for almost all my base meshes, allowing me to establish initial proportions and design sophisticated forms. I create a rig by connecting, moving, and scaling them. By pressing the A key, I can quickly preview how the final mesh will look. When I finish the construction stage, to further develop it and add details, I convert ZSpheres to Adaptive Skin and then low-res PolyMesh.

I use the Move brushes to further develop the shape and proportions of the mesh and start adding details with Clay Brushes, gradually increasing the mesh Subdivision Resolution.

Are you using SpotLight to texture or for sculptural details?

Besides texturing, SpotLight lets me manipulate and combine images before projecting them onto my models. I can texture in a fast and intuitive manner without the need to use external 2D applications to prepare my images. SpotLight is also handy for sculpting details on model surfaces.

When images are loaded into SpotLight, I adapt them to match the size and shape of the object by using the Rotate and Scale functions. To paint textures on the model's surface, I press the Z button to enter Paint mode.

I activate the RGB button, deactivate Zadd, and then adjust the RGB Intensity and Draw Size of the brush and start painting, switching back and forth by using the Z button when I need to change the size or rotation of the source image. When my texture is ready, I switch the SpotLight off by pressing Shift+Z.

In the Masking menu, I choose Mask By Intensity and switch Polypaint > Colorize off. That allows me to add details to the surface with sculpting brushes.

Are you using ZSketch? How?

I use ZSketch to paint armatures. ZSketching can snap onto an existing surface and is good for prototyping and experimenting with new shapes. There are three workflows for ZSketching: I sketch freely in 3D space, use ZSphere's structure as base, or sketch directly onto the SubTool.

Usually I append a ZSphere as a SubTool to my model, activate EditSketch, and start painting structures. The A shortcut helps me preview how the final mesh will look. To finish, I create Unified Skin from it. Increasing Subdivisions Count and Skin Resolution allows me to keep fine details.

ANDRZEJ KUZIOLA

What are some of your time-saving tips when using ZBrush?

I keep old models, meshes, and custom alphas organized in Lightbox for further reuse. Doing that is a great time saver when I don't need to start from scratch and can modify an existing mesh and build a new model based on it.

How has ZBrush helped you to successfully define your own graphic/artistic style?

Thanks to ZBrush, I don't need to sketch out my ideas in 2D software; I can start straight in 3D. My imagination works much better in a 3D environment, where it is much easier for me to design. Tools like ZSpheres, ZSketch, Move, and the Sculpting Brushes allow me to experiment with forms and encourage improvisation. ZBrush eliminates time-consuming, technical aspects of the regular 3D packages and gives the artist an almost real-world clay sculpting experience.

What advice do you have for artists working with ZBrush?

My advice is to save often and as separate files. ZBrush is sophisticated software and uses a system at its maximum level, so it crashes sometimes. It can also corrupt a saved file, though that's not as common.

Experiment with forms, designs, and interesting shapes. ZBrush makes experimentation with forms, designs, and interesting shapes efficient and intuitive, so why not take advantage of it?

ANDRZEJ KUZIOLA

Contact
Edinburgh, United Kingdom ■ kuziola@gmail.com ■ www.kuziola.com

Education/Experience
Graphic Design Certificate at SAE Institute in Glasgow

Awards and Career Highlights
Illustration published in Ballistic Media's *EXPOSE 7* and *EXPOSE 8*. 1st place in The Gnomon Workshop's contest "Ghosts & Ghouls" and "In the Doorway" ■ 1st place in The *.psd Magazine*'s contest "Holiday Memories" ■ 2nd place in 3Dconnexion's 3D Design Challenge: November ■ 2nd place in the CGchannel Digital Sculpting contest: Fallen Angels ■ 2nd place in e-grafik.pl contest "Dark Art"

Client List
MAXON Computer GmbH ■ Ballistic Publishing ■ Imagine Publishing

Hardware/Software Used with ZBrush
Hardware: Mac Pro, MacBook Pro, Wacom Cintiq tablet

Software: Cinema 4D, Photoshop, Silo, Painter, TopoGun, UV Layout

ANDRZEJ KUZIOLA

Gallery

"Sarcofago."

"Ascension."

ANDRZEJ KUZIOLA

"Defeat."

"H2O."

ANDRZEJ KUZIOLA

"Having a Meal—A Conversation with God."

"Holiday to Remember."

ANDRZEJ KUZIOLA

"Parthenogenesis."

"Teddy Bear Snacks."

ANDRZEJ KUZIOLA

ANDRZEJ KUZIOLA

"Virgin's Bottomless Despair."

"Trick or Treat."

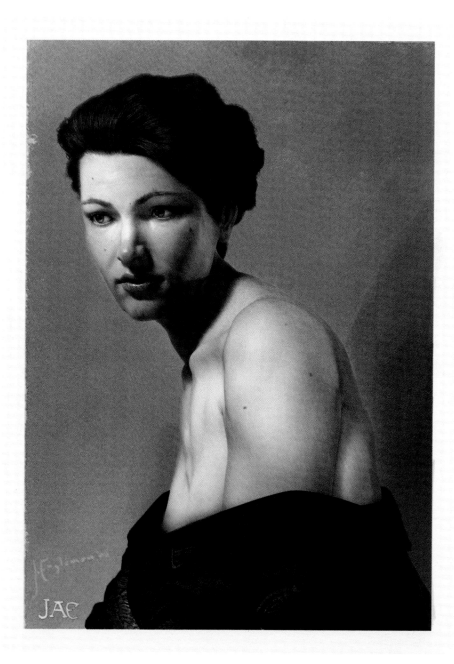

JEREMY ENGLEMAN

About the Artist

I've been a computer graphics professional since 1993. I have experience in games, multimedia, print, and film, and I'm currently employed with DreamWorks Feature Animation as a look development artist. I've worked for many clients, including Sting, Peter Gabriel, Dodge, Penguin-Putnam, Duncan Studio, and Disney. I've developed award-winning projects such as *Vigilante 8*; Leonardo da Vinci's *Codex Leicester*; *Riven*, the sequel to *Myst*; *Patriot*; *Monsters vs Aliens*; and *How to Train Your Dragon*.

Artist's Statement

More is out; less is in. Pushing the low-end boundary of 3D has been a preoccupation of mine for my entire career. I tend to use limits, whether they involve polygon count or time, to achieve a more spontaneous 3D workflow. In this medium, obsession with microscopic detail tends to reign. It's easy to spend weeks on end painting a specular map for human pore structure. In my free time, I like to counter that with a painterly approach, where form is rough and loose, and details are left to the viewer.

"Head of a Woman."

JEREMY ENGLEMAN

Techniques

Technique 1: Achieve a Fully Lit and Textured 3D Gesture Painting from a Live Model in 3+1 Hours

Getting loose with 3D as a medium is something of an oxymoron. It isn't ordinarily an art form that is conducive to quick expression. There's usually far too much overhead involved in the production of a 3D image. But with a little practice and ZBrush, this becomes possible.

To accomplish a finished work in four hours, it helps to know the stages and have time guidelines for each one. I break my workflow into four phases: modeling, texturing, lighting, and post.

Phase 1: Modeling (1½–2 Hours)

1. I use either ZSpheres or a prefab geometry doll as a base mesh. I've used both, but I tend to prefer the geometry doll. See Figure 10.1.

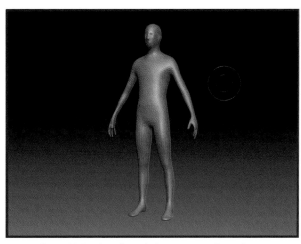

Figure 10.1   A ready-made base saves precious minutes.

2. Using TransPose tool, I pose my base mesh, paying attention to the gesture and movement of the figure. The great thing about a study of this nature is that it's simple to alter and tweak the gesture later; however, it's best to try to get it right from the beginning. I spend a little time measuring with my stylus. It's easier to add the masses and details if the relationships are already in place. See Figure 10.2.

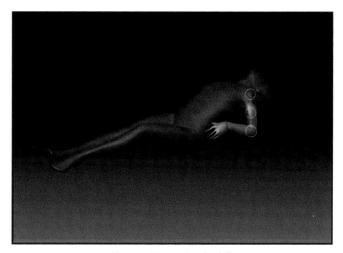

Figure 10.2   Posing the doll.

3. I build the forms and masses. See Figure 10.3.

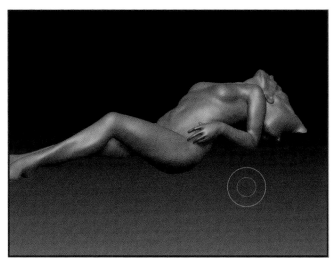

Figure 10.3   Massing it in.

TIP

Avoid dividing the model too much; it will tempt you with details. You can use ZBrush's Posable Symmetry tool even while the model is posed to sculpt the major forms on each side. Think about how the light is hitting all the major planes. You'll want to match that as closely as possible.

4. Once I'm satisfied with the masses, I add the details and gravity. These add the spark of life and realism to the model. It's not necessary to add detail everywhere. I pick an area and focus on that, leaving the rest loose. If there are sufficient details and weight in an appropriate area, and the basic masses are correct, the viewer can fill in the details. See Figure 10.4.

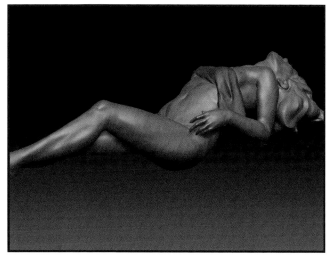

Figure 10.4   Details and weight don't need to be added everywhere.

JEREMY ENGLEMAN

Phase 2: Texturing: (30–45 Minutes)

1. I start with a range of base colors and paint in semitransparent layers. I mimic the layers of skin, beginning with reds, purples, and blues. I build up to yellows, greens, and whites. Finally, I wash in the local skin color. My technique involves a continual process of building and tearing down to create depth and richness. I try not to click Undo. My strokes are deliberate and committed. See Figure 10.5.

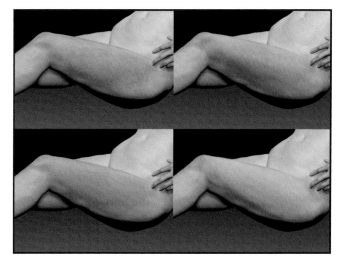

Figure 10.5   Build layers of paint as if you are building layers of skin.

2. I might even leave a little bit of Zadd on the brush. It can accentuate the mass of the form and better reveal the strokes. See Figure 10.6.

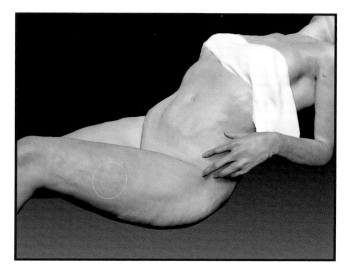

Figure 10.6   Don't be afraid to show the stroke.

3. I might paint in some light and shadow, but I'm careful not to compete with the actual forms. I only accentuate them. See Figure 10.7.

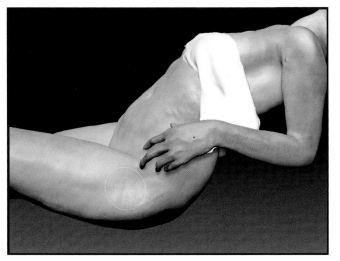

Figure 10.7 Accentuating lighting and form with value and color.

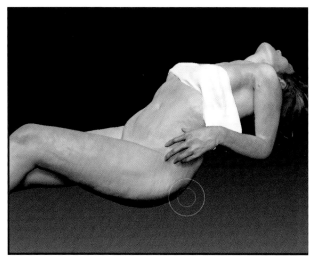

Figure 10.8 Leave something to the imagination.

4. I concentrate on my focal point and leave everything else loose. Viewers like contrast in an image, and in this image the level of detail varies. See Figure 10.8.

TIP

Having an area that is the clear focal point is pleasing to the viewer. An image with the same amount of detail everywhere registers as nothing but noise.

Phase 3: Lighting (30–45 Minutes)

1. I rough in the environment to inform lighting. It should be value and form only. I might polish and texture it later, but at this stage, I simply mass it in to support the piece. See Figure 10.9.

2. I temporarily remove the texture from the model and assign a mid-gray color. I create a range of values that work and keep the lighting simple. It's usually best if there appears to be just one light source and the bounce light. Of course, I try to match the actual light quality falling on the figure, so more than one may be necessary. I ensure there is no clamping to pure white or pure black, striving for a broad range of tonality. See Figure 10.10.

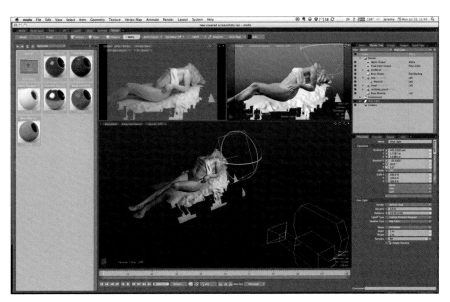

Figure 10.9
A rough environment.

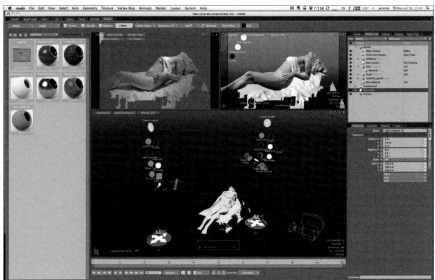

Figure 10.10
Value study.

3. Thinking of lighting in components is valuable. I try to get each part of the total lighting contribution right and then bring them together. Often I rely on simple three-point lighting: key, bounce, and rim. I use whatever kind of shaded ambient light (Final Gather or Global Illumination) my package supports to do the ambient bounce light. I turn that off and position my key light, often a SpotLight, and do the same for the rim light.

Working with them individually helps me isolate and visualize what each part of the lighting is doing. It means I make fewer mistakes, need fewer lights, spin my wheels less, and am able to track down problems more easily when they occur. Once I am satisfied with each component, I turn it on and add it up. Then I adjust light intensities to create balanced relationships between them. See Figure 10.11.

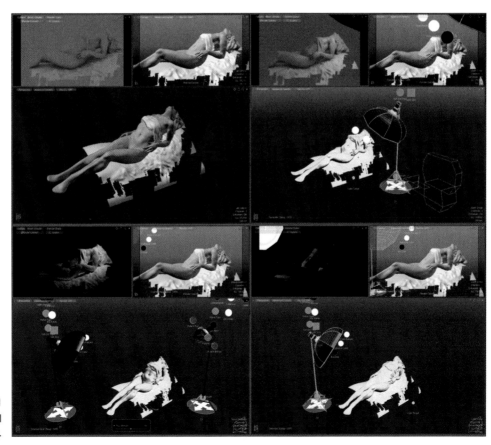

Figure 10.11
Creating and adjusting individual components of the lighting.

JEREMY ENGLEMAN

TIP

Work on each light and its contribution individually so you can better visualize what each part of the lighting is doing. Once you're satisfied, turn each one on and add it up.

4. Once the values are correct, I fold in the color component of the light. First I bring in the texture I've painted. Then I add color to my actual light sources. See Figure 10.12.

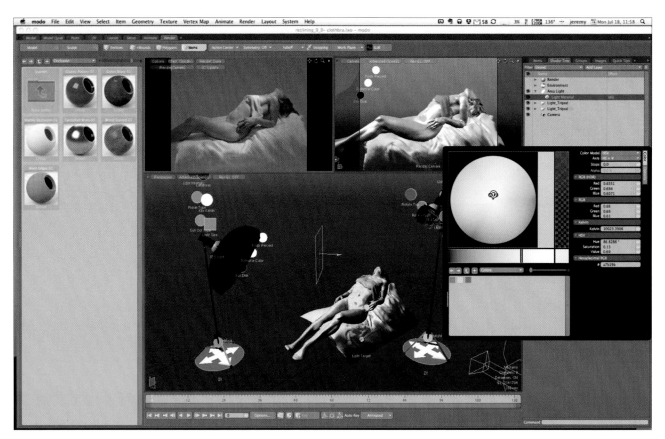

Figure 10.12 Bring the color.

CAUTION

It's easy to spend a lot of time in post, but try to limit yourself. If you take much longer than an hour, there's a danger of overworking and losing the original spontaneity.

Phase 4: Post (Aim for 1 Hour or Less)

1. The stressful part is over! I now spend additional time on the environment and tweak the gesture and flow of the figure. I add some details I may have neglected. This works best when there is variety in amount of detail. I leave some parts strategically rough but add detail to the point of interest. It doesn't have to be perfect. See Figure 10.13.

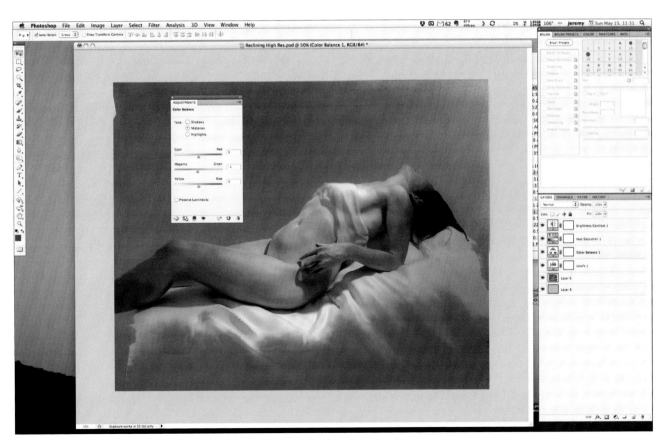

Figure 10.13   Last-chance tweaks.

2. Now I render and process. I bring the final image into Photoshop for some last-minute touches. My changes at this step are simple color-corrects or glares. I add a simple background at this time as well. See Figure 10.14.

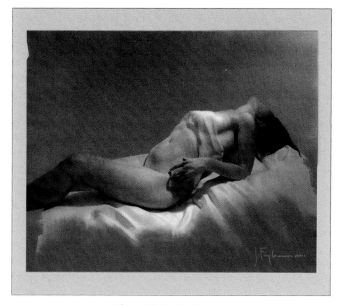

Figure 10.14 Final image.

Often it's a struggle to get everything done in a limited amount of time. But mastering this process leads to a better understanding of what's important. It means spending less time with insignificant details and more time on the most important part of the picture: the gesture and the tone. It also means working faster and more efficiently. The result is a better, more intuitive sense of color and rhythm. Other benefits are eyes and a mind trained so that all of this seamlessly translates to more finished work.

Insights
Q&A

What motivates you or your work?

I'm thrilled by the challenge of inventing, discovering, and learning. Whether it's a novel technique, an acute observation, or a happy accident, the eventual promise of epiphany is worth creative struggle.

Who/what are your inspirations and influences?

So much inspires me: old men and young women; alleys and abandoned things; power lines; road trips; NASA; scientists and cobblers; train stations; small-town parades; Utah, the middle-child of the United States; middle-children; Legos; wood paneling.

I'm inspired every day by so many of my coworkers at DreamWorks Animation. The quantity of incredible artwork done by hundreds of people every day is humbling, and I'm fortunate to be counted among those artists.

Which artists do you admire? Why?

I admire John Register for his quiet solitude, Thomas Eakins for his marriage of science and art, Rembrandt and Vermeer for recording living light in pigment, William Eggleston for his sublimation of the commonplace, Henri Cartier-Bresson for perfecting composition, André Kertész for his sense of humor, Eliott Erwitt for framing moments otherwise lost, Jacob Collins for his studious superhuman precision, and Jeremy Lipking for the spectacular skin in his paintings.

When did you start using ZBrush?

I started using ZBrush regularly around 2006. I had seen it in 2005 and even attempted to use it, but I wasn't able to understand it until 2006.

Describe your creative process and workflow. How does ZBrush fit?

I go to live figure model sessions with a group of oil painters and do three-hour studies. I attempt to sculpt the geometry, paint the texture, and then light the model within that time frame. I spend another hour or so afterward tweaking, cleaning up, or finishing neglected areas. I've tried to engage in this process without ZBrush, and let me tell you, ZBrush makes all the difference.

What's your workflow? Do you create from scratch with ZSpheres or import geometry from another package to work on/develop?

I've tried both creating from scratch in ZBrush with ZSpheres as well as importing geometry. I love the idea of ZSpheres, and before the addition of the Transpose tool, I used them extensively. However, transposing a low-res mummy-doll is my current workflow of choice.

What are some of your favorite ZBrush features? How do you use them?

Transpose is one of my favorites. It really enables me to get the gesture of the figure right, even preserving details after they have been added. This is something that simply isn't possible with traditional paint.

Polypaint is another favorite of mine. It has minimized my need to deal with UVs, and who can't appreciate that?

I'll make the Socratic admission that in ZBrush, as in life, all I know is that I know nothing. ZBrush is such a confoundingly profound software package that knowing it is an art form. Mastering ZBrush is the computer graphics (CG) equivalent of throwing a needle through a sheet of glass or catching a fly with chopsticks.

Are you using any of the new brushes in ZBrush, like the Move Elastic Brush?

Yes, Move Elastic is the bomb. I also really dig Clay Tubes, and I've made a custom variant of Pen Fur that I like quite a bit.

What tools do you most often use to texture? SpotLight? Image Plane? Projection Master? ZAppLink?

For my studies, I paint all my textures with the standard brushes in Polypaint mode. Although it's still ideal to have a properly UV'd model, it's absolute bliss not to have to deal with them. Polypaint does the job in my particular application of ZBrush, since I'm pretty loose with my color and detail. I don't generally zoom in to the pore level, and when I do I tend to use another package. The drudgery of UVs is the biggest creative buzzkill. The genius of Polypaint is that the initial creative spark of immediate paint can be converted and preserved once the model is UV'd.

What advice do you have for artists working with ZBrush?

Despite its unconventional, bordering on bizarre, user interface paradigm, working in ZBrush eventually becomes fluid. I'd advise new users to create a cheat sheet of how you do everything. It has so many great features, but they are often buried and obfuscated by requiring an arcane sequence of steps or hotkeys to accomplish. It's easy to get lost, but if you make a trail of breadcrumbs, you'll find the interface actually does begin to make sense. But don't stop using ZBrush for more than two weeks; you'll completely forget how to do things.

What do you wish someone had told you when you started with ZBrush?

Stick with it; it's around for the long haul.

How has ZBrush helped you successfully define your own graphic/artistic style?

ZBrush has most helped me pursue my dream of mating CG with academic figure studies. This would be next to impossible without it.

JEREMY ENGLEMAN

Resources

Links

- http://www.thegnomonworkshop.com/
- http://www.deviantart.com/
- http://www.posespace.com/
- http://yubnub.org/

JEREMY ENGLEMAN

Studio

DreamWorks Feature Animation

Contact

Jeremy Engleman ■ Glendale, California, USA ■ j.engleman@yahoo.com ■ http://jeremyengleman.deviantart.com/

Education/Experience

My BFA from the University of Colorado is TBD. Or maybe DOA.

Awards and Career Highlights

Gnomon Gallery, an exhibit of holograms by 12 top 3D artists: 2008

The Best of 3D Graphics, Images included in the book published by Epic: 2002

3D World, two-page portfolio spread: 2000

Computer Arts, two-page portfolio spread: 2000

Science Exhibit, Museum Victoria, Texture Photographs: 1999. Melbourne, Australia

Digital Art, The Center for Digital Art and Nexus Gallery: 1999. New York, New York

Digital Art in a Traditional World, Long Beach Arts: 1999. Long Beach, California

Computer Graphics World, two-page portfolio spread: June 1999

3D Design Big Kahuna award, Nominee-Print Graphics: 1998

Computer Graphics World, Online Image of the Month: June 1996

MSA-Realsoft Japan 3D competition, Third Place-Animation: 1996. Tokyo, Japan

Four Cameras, a four-person show at Rock Arts Gallery: 1993. Denver, Colorado

Auraria Photofest, Honorable Mention: 1992. Denver, Colorado

Client List

DreamWorks, Disney, Duncan Studio, Luxoflux, Activision, ESPN, Dodge, Cyan, Corbis

Hardware/Software Used with ZBrush

Hardware: MacBook Pro, a little 4×5 Wacom tablet, and a big lap desk

Software: These days I generally stick to ZBrush, Modo, and Photoshop

Gallery

"Nape of a Woman's Neck."

JEREMY ENGLEMAN

"Procedurally Shaded Plums."

"Procedurally Shaded Sushi."

JEREMY ENGLEMAN

"Blinn Bottles."

"Bonnie: 3-Hour Figure Study."

JEREMY ENGLEMAN

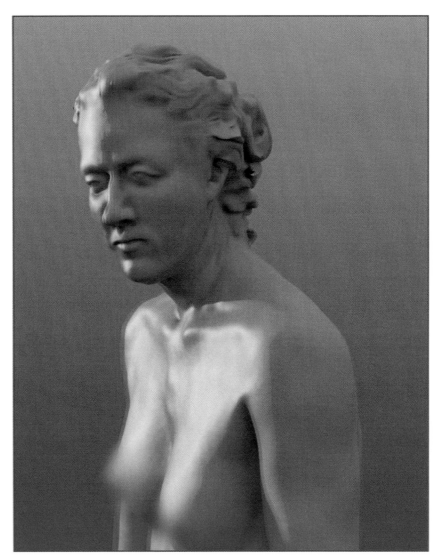

"Bust: 3-Hour Live Model Sculpt in Stereo."

"Melissa: 3-Hour Figure Study."

"Dreamworks Promenade: 3D Outdoor Sketch."

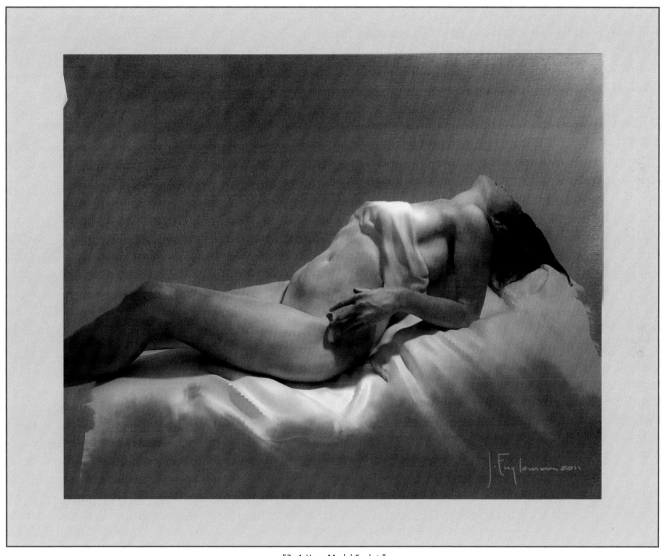

"3+1 Hour Model Sculpt."

CHRIS NICHOLS

About the Artist

Upon graduation from high school in Vancouver, Canada, I did three years of graphic design and was introduced to digital art. I learned Photoshop and a bit of Cinema 4D, and I knew I wanted to get more involved in 3D. In 2004, I did a year of animation at the same college, but the course was underdeveloped, and we had to source outside help to come in and teach us. We tried to make a faux episode of *Animatrix* as a year-long project, but the class shrank to me and another guy by the end of the year. The two of us set up my apartment like a small studio and worked day and night. I learned a lot about modeling and texturing from him and my work on the film.

We never finished the film, but we had enough material to create a sort of trailer, so we flew over to Sydney, Australia, and showed our work to several studios. We had a good response and received some helpful critiques. We even got to do some short-term work at Digital Pictures. From there, we were hired closer to home to work on a short film called *Ironbird* for almost a year before we decided to move to Vancouver to look for work. In 2007, I ended up working as a modeler at Bardel Entertainment, and my friend was hired at Blur in Venice. After four years, I'm still in Vancouver, having worked at Bardel, Spin VFX, Method/CIS, and now Digital Domain as a modeler/texturer and concept artist.

Artist's Statement

It's important to have a solid foundation in visual art. Taking three years of design prepared me for my career in visual effects (VFX). Understanding shape, form, and color is vital to being a successful modeler or texturer in this industry. The real secret to getting better is practice. Ever since I began professionally five years ago, I've been working on my own projects to help me become a faster, more expressive, and better-skilled artist.

"Tortoise."

Techniques

Technique 1: How to Sculpt Wrinkled Skin

1. I like to start by turning off all the SubTools in the scene except for the piece I'm about to detail. In this case, I begin detailing the neck, sculpting in skin folds and wrinkles/scales.

I like to have a reference handy, so on my other screen I have several close-up images of turtle and tortoise skin so I can get an idea of what to strive for. See Figure 11.1.

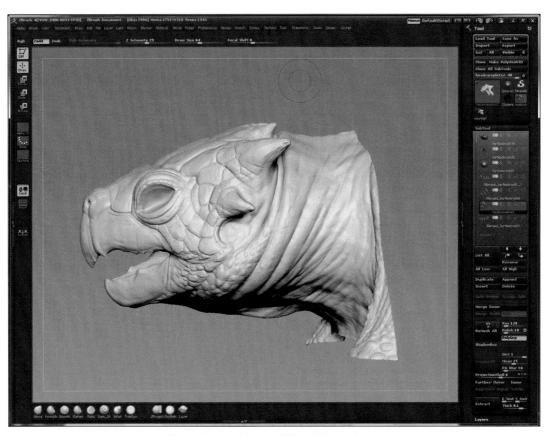

Figure 11.1 Isolate area of ZTools before sculpting.

2. Once I've isolated the area using the Hide tool (Ctrl+Shift drag on area), I block in the broad strokes with the Clay Buildup Brush. I'm only interested in building up my forms, not putting in any real detail or skin texture. I set the brush intensity to 10–15 and the focal shift to –8, and I start blocking out skin detail.

The trick to this is zooming in and out of the sculpt and analyzing how the forms are working with the overall area. I sculpt in shapes with a focus on the direction of their flow and then build up those areas until I'm getting some nice wrinkles happening. Then I lightly smooth it all out using the Shift key. See Figure 11.2.

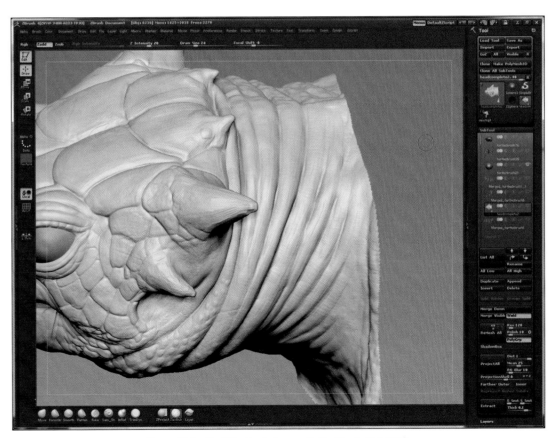

Figure 11.2 Start blocking in forms with the Clay Buildup Brush.

CHRIS NICHOLS

3. Another technique I like to work into my process is masking off where wrinkles intersect by holding down the Ctrl key and painting a mask. I hold down Shift and click on the area to soften the mask. Then I switch to the Move Brush, setting my intensity to something low like 5–10 and then gently pushing the unmasked area closer to the masked-off part. I Ctrl-click the background to reverse the mask and then move that unmasked area closer to the mask. This creates a nice crease where the wrinkles meet, adding to the wrinkle effect. See Figure 11.3.

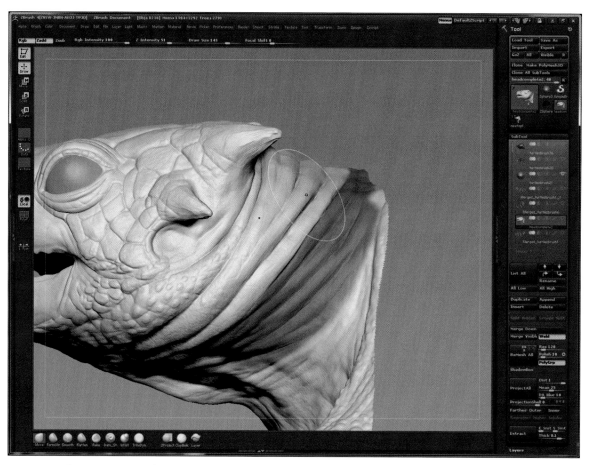

Figure 11.3   Mask off an area starting at the crease and use the Move Brush to push wrinkles closer to each other.

4. I'm happy with how the skin folds are working, so I start to sculpt in some of the bumpy surfaces using my Clay Buildup Brush again. I set it to a fairly low intensity and work up little bumps all over the surface, diversifying them in scale.

I use the Shift key to smooth them out and integrate them into the wrinkle. I repeat this over and over until I get a nice uneven surface that looks organic. See Figure 11.4.

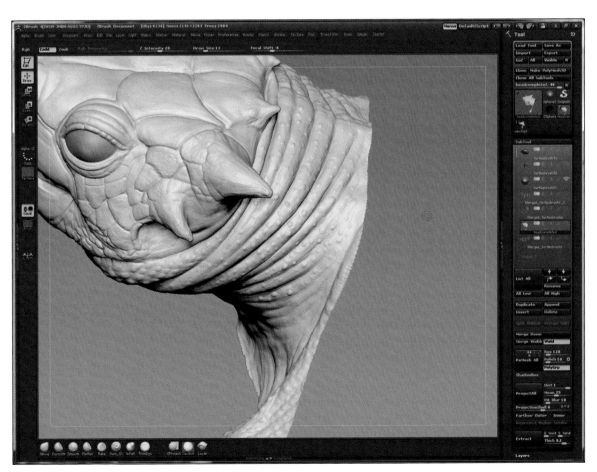

Figure 11.4 Add rough details with the Clay Buildup Brush.

5. For some of the final detailing, I switch to the Dam Standard Brush and set the intensity to 7. With a smallish scale, I draw random lines over the wrinkles, starting from the crease and ending a few wrinkles over in a horizontal fashion. I like to draw from one side to the other—whatever looks good.

Then I switch back to the Clay Buildup Brush and lightly sculpt up the areas close to the lines, in random areas. That seems to enhance the shapes and add contrast to the lines. After that, I draw circles around some of the bumps with the Dam Standard Brush to refine the shapes a bit. See Figure 11.5.

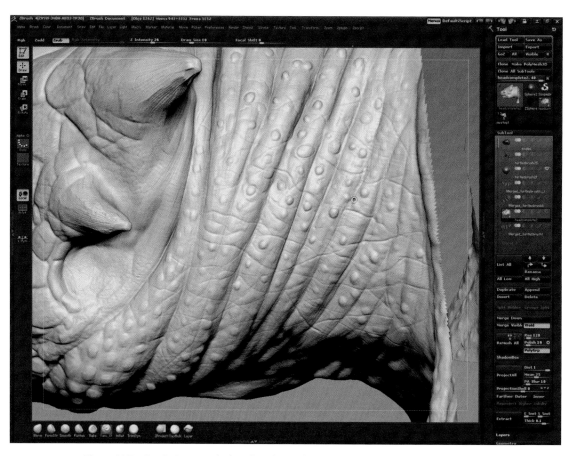

Figure 11.5 Use the Dam Standard Brush to draw in fine wrinkles and outline bumps for definition.

6. I like to go over the area with the Clay Buildup Brush until all the shapes are working nicely together from a distance, smoothing out some areas of detail so they don't stand out so much.

Also at this point, I might see which area I want to focus on to bring out even more detail, as long as it reads well as a whole. See Figure 11.6 for the final image.

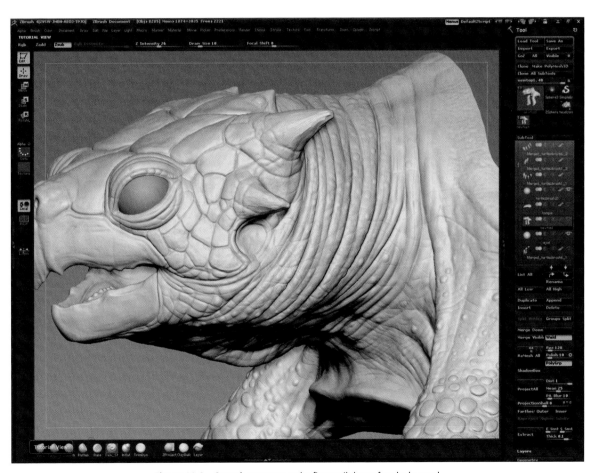

Figure 11.6   Smooth out areas and refine until the surface looks good.

Technique 2: How to Sculpt Scales

1. Starting with the detailing of the leg, I roughly block out where the scales are going to fit in the sculpt, using the Dam Standard Brush to draw lines across the surface and then inflating the inside shapes with the Clay Buildup Brush. Again, I'm referencing photos of different tortoise scale structures for inspiration. See Figure 11.7.

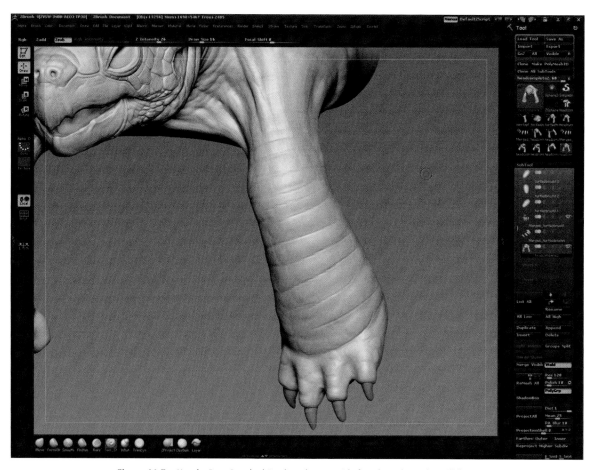

Figure 11.7　Use the Dam Standard Brush to draw a guide for where the scales will flow.

2. I use the Dam Standard Brush to draw in where I'm going to sculpt out the scales on the surface. I don't spend a lot of time on this; I just want a rough guide of where to place them, and then I can zoom in and out to see how they're working together. An irregular offset pattern works quite well. See Figure 11.8.

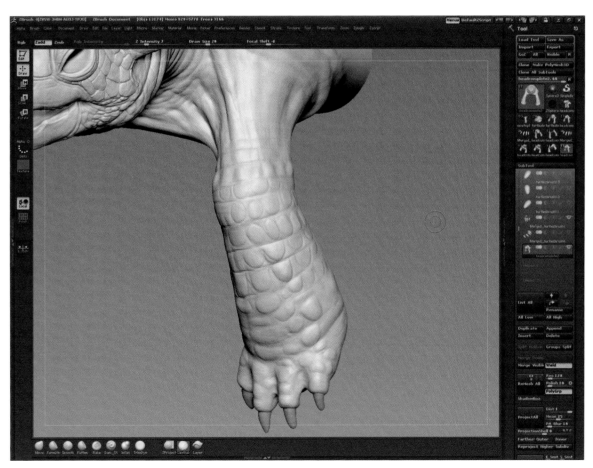

Figure 11.8 Draw in a guide for where scales will sit on the surface.

3. Now I really block out the scale structure. Using my Clay Buildup Brush again, I go over the area where I outlined scales to give them volume. I often switch over to my Move Brush to pull the scales out slightly and give shape to the silhouette. See Figure 11.9.

4. Once the scales are in place and I'm happy with the layout, I refine them slightly by using my TrimDynamic Brush to flatten out the scales and define the edges. Using my Dam Standard Brush, I outline the scales so they are bolder and feel slightly disconnected from the leg skin. See Figure 11.10.

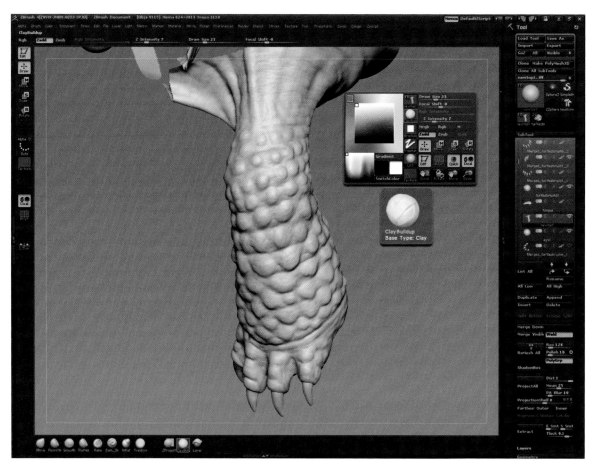

Figure 11.9 Use the Clay Buildup Brush to rough in the scales. Switch over to the Move Brush to pull the forms out.

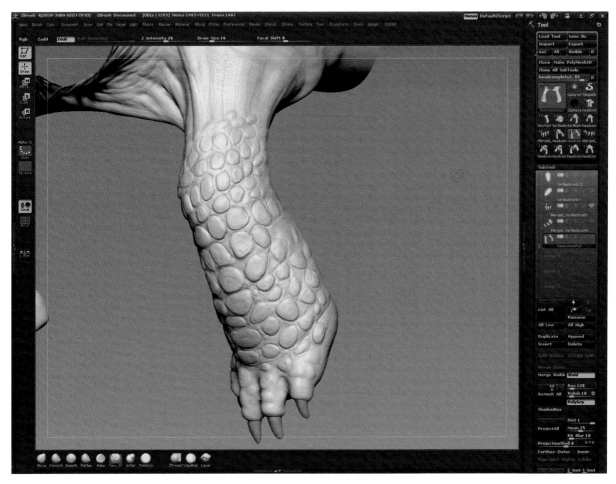

Figure 11.10   Start to refine the scales using the TrimDynamic Brush to flatten out the scales and give them a harder edge.

5. I continue to use my Dam Standard and Clay Buildup Brushes to add bits of detail to the scales by sculpting the interior in a circular pattern in relation to the scale shape.

I like to spend time refining each scale and the surrounding skin to create a distinct separation between the surfaces. See Figure 11.11.

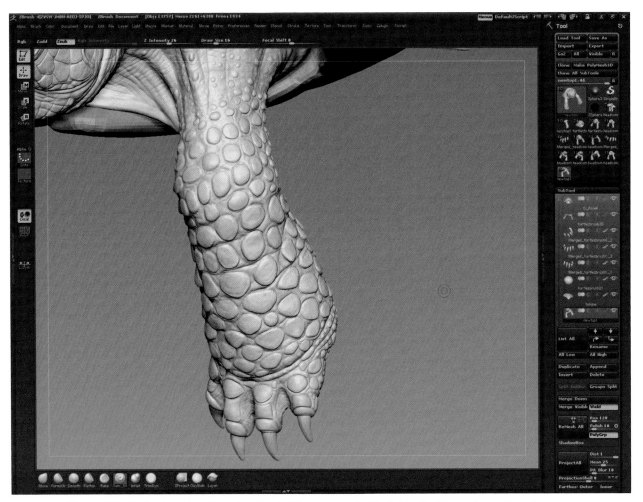

Figure 11.11   Define the scales with the Dam Standard Brush and use the Clay Buildup Brush to roughen up the surfaces a bit.

Insights

Q&A

What motivates you or your work?

Reality inspires me. When I feel nothing interesting is being created anymore, I return to nature photography for inspiration. I really love surface textures and details, so anything amphibian or reptilian gives me ideas and inspiration for my own projects.

Who/what are your inspirations and influences?

I love psychedelic stuff. Films like *2001: A Space Odyssey* and *Enter the Void* have trance-like imagery that stimulates my mind.

Which artists do you admire? Why?

I admire the art of Carlos Huante and Zdzislaw Beksinski. Lately I've been getting into *Warhammer 40,000* and can't get enough Adrian Smith and John Blanche art. Expressive artists who can tell a story with their work are so interesting.

When did you start using ZBrush?

In 2004, a friend showed me some videos of Martin Krol making an angler fish in ZBrush 2.0, and we started using it on our short film at school. Initially, I used it only to paint textures, but later I did the bump maps and sculpting in the package. Now I work 80% of the time in ZBrush.

Describe your creative process and workflow. How does ZBrush fit?

I usually start modeling in Maya. I create a basic shape with fairly clean topology and take that into ZBrush and start blocking out the basic forms with the Clay Buildup Brush. After I get my general shapes, I refine them to a point where I'm fighting against the mesh and need to retopologize my model.

I either use ZBrush's Topology tools for this or export an object to TopoGun. Having retopologized the surface, I import that as a new SubTool into ZBrush and use projection to transfer all the details from the old SubTool to the new one. I refine further, possibly adding more levels to the SubTool and defining with the Clay Buildup, Dam Standard, and Move Brushes. When I'm at my highest level and all my large- and mid-frequency shapes are finished, I sometimes use Lightbox and different alphas to paint on finer details. Once the model is complete, I generally use the UV Master plug-in to create my UVs and then Decimation Master to create a detailed yet lighter model, ready for texturing.

What's your workflow? Do you create from scratch with ZSpheres or import geometry from another package to work on/develop?

I generally start from a mesh I made in Maya unless it's something simple, in which case I start from a sphere or cube in ZBrush. Sometimes I also use ZSpheres for things like branches or trees.

What are some of your favorite ZBrush features? How do you use them?

With every new version of ZBrush, my techniques change slightly. I began using the Clay Buildup Brush constantly in ZBrush 4, and now it's my main brush for blocking out shape. I love the way it gives the surface an uneven, organic surface, so it's particularly useful for sculpting creatures. Decimation Master is also essential in both my personal and professional pipeline. Being able to export a light mesh with all the sculpting details and my UVs intact is extremely useful when it comes to texturing in other packages like Mari, or even the final render in Maya.

CHRIS NICHOLS

CHRIS NICHOLS

The ProjectAll feature in ZBrush is such a powerful tool when it comes to extracting detail from a cyberscan or transferring details from one mesh to another. Both are huge parts of my pipeline.

How are you using TimeLine?
I like to use TimeLine to set up my sculpting or rendering cameras. This allows me to snap back to it when I need to.

Are you using SpotLight to texture or for sculptural details?
Yes, I'm using SpotLight for sculptural details; it's intuitive and fast. It's a great way of painting details onto a surface using alphas. I love the way the textured images are organized to keep the screen space clear but my options visible.

Are you using any of the new brushes in ZBrush, like the Move Elastic Brush?
I swapped over the Inflate Brush for the Clay Buildup Brush, which I use for almost everything.

What are you using for hard edge modeling?
The TrimDynamic Brush is my favorite for this. I never use the Flatten Brush anymore.

Which ZPlugs do you use? How?
I use Transpose for posing the model and Decimation Master for exporting high-res meshes with UVs intact for textures and rendering. Also, the Multi Map Exporter is perfect for baking out displacement maps with multiple UV shells.

What are your favorite new sculpting tools?
Clay Buildup Brush is my favorite. It really feels like sculpting with clay.

What advice do you have for artists working with ZBrush?
My advice would be to really explore what's possible with the brushes. Fantastic effects are within reach by experimenting with the Flakes and Fracture Brushes together. Try to get as much detail out of each subdivision level before you up the resolution.

What do you wish someone had told you when you started with ZBrush?
I wish someone had told me not to worry about bringing in an animation mesh to ZBrush. I've found it's best to just bring in a simple mesh with edge loops where I need them for sculpt resolution.

Resources

Links

- www.cgfeedback.com
- www.digitaldomain.com
- www.kolbyjukes.com
- http://vimmy.cgsociety.org/gallery

CHRIS NICHOLS

Contact

Chris Nichols ▪ Burnaby, B.C. Canada ▪
porkpiesamurai@gmail.com ▪ www.digitalarttutorials.com

Studio

www.porkpiesamurai.com

Education/Experience

Advanced diploma of motion graphics and graphic design

Awards and Career Highlights

CGTalk award, 3D Total awards, Expose, *3D Artist* magazine
article and cover, ZBrush Central, ZBrush Vancouver event
speaker, cofounder of annual CG event in Vancouver
"Anomaly," SIGGRAPH ZBrush presentation

Client List

Ironbird Films, Whizz Digital, Bardel Entertainment, Spin
VFX, CIS/Method Vancouver, Digital Domain, and Axis
Animation

Hardware/Software Used with ZBrush

Hardware: Intel i7 970 2.67GHz with 6GB RAM and an
NVIDIA GTX 470

Software: Maya and Mari

CHRIS NICHOLS

Gallery

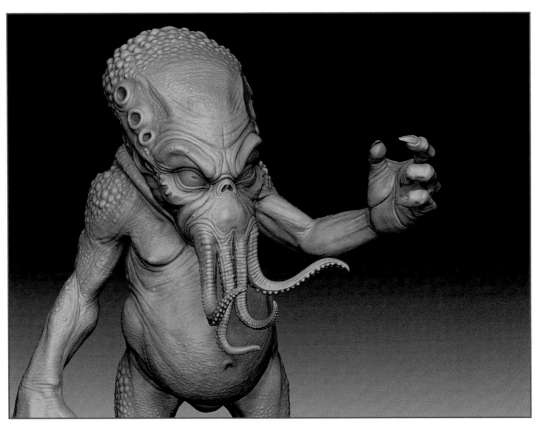

"Cthulhu."

"Cthulhu Final."

CHRIS NICHOLS

"Gentleman."

"Gentleman Final."

"Hatch."

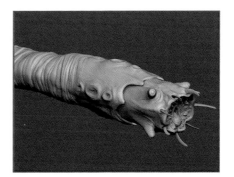

"Revulsion."

CHRIS NICHOLS

"Gunslinger."

"Merc."

ALEXEY KASHPERSKY

About the Artist

This chapter was translated to English from Russian.

I was born in Poltava, Ukraine. I graduated with an artistic streak from Poltava Lyceum #1. I entered the Poltava National Technical University, specializing in fine and decorative arts. Several years later, I earned a master of fine arts with honors.

I became interested in computer graphics 16 years ago and have continued to work in that field. In 2007, I founded the site ARTTalk.ru, where I work now. Sometimes I undertake interesting freelance projects, too. My hobbies are sports and music, and my favorite subjects are sculpture, drawing, and anatomy.

Artist's Statement

I fully share the idea that although every artist could paint a door, not every painter can draw a painting. Likewise, to become a computer graphics (CG) artist, it's not enough to know how to use the programs or have the technical skills; you also have to be an artist. You have to learn to feel the flow and melody of every line in every curve because there's no button on the computer you can click to "make beautiful."

"Atlantis Herald."

Techniques

Technique 1: Making Water Splash in ZBrush

I want to share with you the secret of how I modeled the wave in my work "Dream" found on page 233. I've had so many questions about it. I don't create water with plug-ins; I model all of it by hand, with polygons and spheres. To do that, I accurately re-create the waveform that I've imagined. See Figure 12.1.

1. Extrude the mesh you want to form the body of the model. See Figure 12.2.

2. Because the density of the mesh was too high for this stage of the work, I've retopologized and continued to form the silhouette of water in 3ds Max. See Figure 12.3.

3. Next, I refine it and make the transition from water to a piece of cloth. See Figure 12.4.

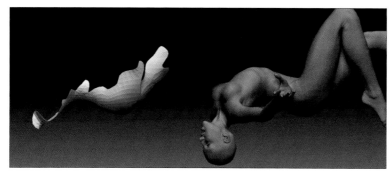

Figure 12.1 Extruding the waveform from the base mesh.

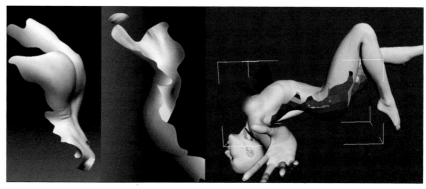

Figure 12.2 Refinement of the waveform.

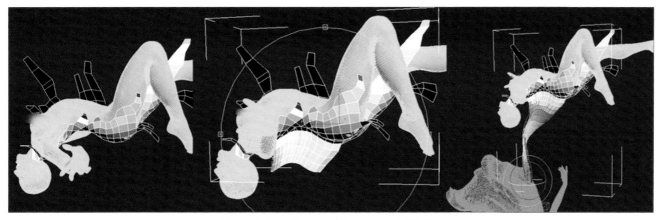

Figure 12.3   Refinement of the waveform in 3ds Max.

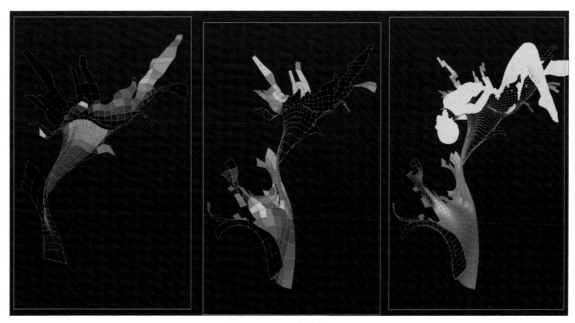

Figure 12.4   Final of this stage.

ALEXEY KASHPERSKY

4. Here is where the fun starts. I add and arrange the 3,000 spheres in their own place in three dimensions for the bubbles. Notice the different size of spheres in Figure 12.5.

Here is a lovely splash resulting from the actions. Most of the work is done, but I now need to turn the topology into the water. To do this, I export the mesh into the file format .obj and upload it to ZBrush.

Figure 12.5 Creating a splash from the sphere.

5. In ZBrush, I use the Unified Skin Tool with maximum detail and minimal smoothing. After that, I go over the entire surface with the Smooth Brush. It is impossible to apply the initial smoothing without losing dozens of small details.

Running smoothing manually takes 10 times longer, but I'm able to preserve all the necessary details, and I have full control. See Figure 12.6.

Figure 12.6 Transfer to ZBrush.

ALEXEY KASHPERSKY

In the end, I create a beautiful waveform. See Figure 12.7.

Figure 12.7   The final model of the wave.

Insights

Q&A

What motivates you or your work?

My need for self-expression and my desire to develop and grow with each creation motivates me.

Who/what are your inspirations and influences?

Nature inspires me. It is perfect in its forms.

Which artists do you admire? Why?

Boris Vallejo is my favorite artist. I recently received positive feedback from him and his wife about my work, which is the great incentive for me. Now I'll work on myself twice as hard.

When did you start using ZBrush?

I think it was 2006 when I discovered ZBrush.

Describe your creative process and workflow. How does ZBrush fit?

Even the smallest work starts with finding references. When it comes to modeling and anatomy, I look for a dozen other photo references. Then I start work in ZBrush. I either create a blank in 3ds Max or use a ZSphere; then I slowly dial the desired shape and volume. I gradually turn to the detail of the model. Sometimes in the creation process, the model needs to be retopologized. This is a tedious process.

But after that, depending on the task, I either texture the model and throw it in 3ds Max for rendering and subsequent work, or finish at this stage if I need it for a 3D printer.

What's your workflow? Do you create from scratch with ZSpheres or import geometry from another package to work on/develop?

It depends on my mood and the task at hand. If it's a quick 3D sketch, I do it directly in ZBrush. If I need a fundamental approach with the correct topology, I create a piece in 3ds Max. Sometimes I just create a retopology model in ZBrush.

What are some of your favorite ZBrush features? How do you use them?

The tool I use most frequently is TransPose. It gives the model the correct posture and form.

Are you using ShadowBox to make base meshes? How?

ShadowBox is a useful tool. It allows me to create an accurate model with a sketch or photo, as previously done in 3ds Max, using planes with Left and Right textures.

Are you using Photoshop overlay for your final image?

Postprocessing in Photoshop makes my job much easier. I think of it as feeding my model and creating an atmosphere of work.

Which ZPlugs do you use? How?

I use two plug-ins: Decimation Master and UV Master. The first is indispensable for reducing the polygon count of a model that makes much of its export to 3ds Max for later manipulation. UV Master is a great tool for creating user-friendly scanner cards, which are easy to adjust in Photoshop.

What are your favorite new sculpting tools?

I don't know about the new sculpting tools, but I usually use Move, Inflat, Standard, and Slash Brushes. Usually they are enough.

ALEXEY KASHPERSKY

What are some of your time-saving tips when using ZBrush?

I highly recommend learning anatomy before sculpting a person or animal. Knowledge is the best way to save time.

What advice do you have for artists working with ZBrush?

It is vital for artists to constantly evolve and have a large knowledge base. My advice to them is to remain curious and never cease their development. Any stop is a regression. The technical skills in ZBrush will evolve with time. Curiosity and creativity are traits that artists should never lose.

How has ZBrush helped you successfully define your own graphic/artistic style?

ZBrush has become an indispensable tool. I can't imagine working without it!

Resources

Links

- www.CGSociety.com
- www.3DTotal.com
- www.CGHub.com
- www.ARTTalk.ru
- www.ZBrushCentral.com

ALEXEY KASHPERSKY

Contact
rid@ArtTalk.ru (email) ▪ www.rid.ArtTalk.ru (website) ▪ twitter.com/ArtTalkRu (Twitter)

Studio
www.ArtTalk.ru

Education/Experience
Masters of fine arts with honors

Awards and Career Highlights
CGSociety.com, Render.ru, 3DTotal.com, CGHub.com, ZBrushCentral.com, DeviantART Daily Selection, Itsartmag.com

Hardware/Software Used with ZBrush
Hardware: 19-inch and 27-inch monitors, Wacom tablet, GeForce GTX295 video card, Core i7-920 processor with DDR3 (1866MHz) RAM running OCZ Platinum Edition 4×3, Rampage II Extreme motherboard

Software: 3ds Max, Mental Ray, Photoshop

Gallery

"Dream."

ALEXEY KASHPERSKY

"Furia."

ALEXEY KASHPERSKY

"Igneon."

ALEXEY KASHPERSKY

"The Guards."

"Vase."

STEFANO DUBAY

About the Artist

My name is Stefano Dubay, and I am from Rome, Italy.

Art and science have always been the driving forces in my creative career, though not always in full agreement until I finished my bachelor's degree in mathematics. That's when I found that visual effects was the perfect way to join both.

I find visual effects challenging and rewarding because it allows me to communicate creatively while being in a constant problem-solving state, looking for ways to facilitate the process and possibly eliminate redundant tasks by automation.

My big breakthrough happened when I decided to enroll in Gnomon School of Visual Effects, where I received 360-degree training in the technical aspect of the craft as well as an insight of what I preferred to do as an artist. I knew I wanted to work in character development from the beginning, although I had never had formal training in art before.

While I was still in school, I had the opportunity to work at Gentle Giant studios for a couple of years. This experience helped me connect all the different skills. I learned how to use a lot of different software to create and edit high-density models in an efficient way. In the meantime, I perfected my sculpting and learned how to scan in 3D. Probably the most important skill I learned there is how to efficiently work as a team on projects. Gentle Giant is also a hybrid digital/traditional sculpting studio, where I got to know and learn from several traditional sculptors what it meant to sculpt traditionally.

All these things helped me when I got into the movie industry working at Rhythm and Hues on *Land of the Lost*. I integrated ZBrush in the production pipeline, creating digital maquettes and developing techniques to obtain dense surface details.

I then spent a year working as a modeling lead at Psyop, Inc. in Venice, where I tweaked and refined my technique to work in a commercial production environment, which, by necessity, is time constrained and challenging.

After that I went back to movie production, joining Sony Pictures Imageworks as a character artist for its upcoming animated feature *Arthur Christmas* created in collaboration with Aardman. (Just think Wallace and Gromit!) The movie comes out the end of 2011. At Sony Pictures Imageworks, I learned to work in a much bigger production facility with a preexisting pipeline that was rigidly set. Even more importantly, I learned what stylization means in the design of a cartoon character. Simplicity is a real challenge when there's no detail to rely upon to distract from the quality of the primary shapes that in the end make up the majority of a character and its visual appeal.

I am soon going to start at Disney Animation Studio in Burbank as a digital character sculptor/modeler.

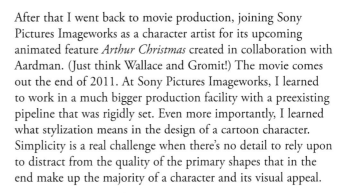

"Formic."

Artist's Statement

Everything I have done so far has developed me as an artist; brick-by-brick building is what I need to exist as a fine artist who works with visual effects. My current goal is applying the power of creation and expressing myself as an individual in every artistic symbol I create.

I've always liked the symbolism that exists behind a well-created piece of art. The skill of the artist is to convey all meaning in a clear fashion. This universal quality of the piece of art is what makes it such a powerful tool of communication. Symbolism can be applied in everything; it doesn't matter if the art is of a creature, a portrait, or a character.

Symbolism doesn't have to be explicit; it can be conveyed by choosing one color palette over another, creating the expression of the eyes in a portrait, or hybridizing different animals to create another being. What ultimately interests me is using such symbols creatively and originally, building a puzzle for the viewer to solve.

Techniques

Technique 1: Formic Project

Reading is one of my favorite hobbies and is a source of endless inspiration. Images blossom in the mind following the written text.

One of the books I love is *Ender's Game*, so I decided to create a Formic drone to explain my process.

1. I start with the usual gathering of reference images that might be useful in the design. In this case, I also have a clear description of this creature from the author, Orson Scott Card.

   The creature had to be reminiscent of an ant but altogether different. The guidelines indicated that it was an endoskeleton but also had the anatomic construction of a bug, with a head, a middle section, and an abdomen. It also had to be able to handle tools and look "intelligent" even if it's not. (All the drones are guided remotely by the central mind of the Formic Queen.) See Figure 13.1.

Figure 13.1 Reference images gathered for the creature.

2. I spend some time browsing the Internet looking for some image that works with the general idea I have in mind. I then start brainstorming a few sketches to sort out my ideas, see what graphically works and what doesn't, and roughly figure out how the creature operates. I especially like inventing the physiology and finding analogs between the things I blend (in this case an ant and elements of human anatomy). I like freedom when developing 3D sketches. I don't really think about topology UVs or anything like that. ZBrush's toolset becomes an essential asset because it allows me to use simple geometries and sculpt them into more complex shapes. For this project, I am essentially using cubes warped as needed, using GoZ if I have to increase the numbers of divisions in one or the other directions because of excessive stretching. See Figure 13.2.

3. Here I am blocking in the head made out of cubes. Even the eyes are smoothed cubes. I usually start from the head, because it conveys more of the character of the creature than the rest of the body. It is also quicker to make less anatomically constrained subjects.

I use ShadowBox to create the base shape of the jaw; it's an awesome tool to quickly create custom-shaped geometries. See Figure 13.3.

Figure 13.2 Brainstorming and design studies.

TIP

Avoid using spheres. Using Transpose Master or other plug-ins' poles (vertices with more than four edges in them) tears the geometry when you import the image back in. Smoothed cubes approximate spheres well enough for my needs here, but I can always replace them with spheres later.

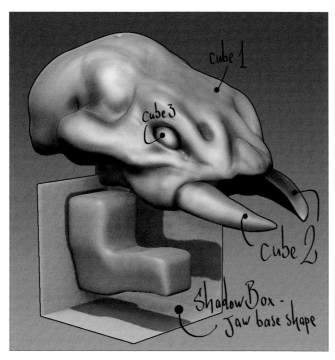

Figure 13.3 Blocking in the head from a few basic
and custom-made objects with ShadowBox.

4. I block the whole creature the same way. Later I'll blend
the overlapping areas using the Clay or Clay Tubes Brush
to smooth out the transition between the separate chunks.
Another technique I recently learned is to combine SubTools
and blend them using the unified skin function in ZBrush.
That creates a new geometry with the same volume. Voxels
works in a similar fashion. It is hard to obtain predictable
results, though, and the blended objects are heavy and
topologically messy.

I like using small chunks to build things up, though,
because I can easily edit sections of the model with
SubTool Master, mirroring and merging whole sections.

One advantage is not having a topology that encapsulates
details into edge loops, because the polycount tends to
climb pretty quickly. Keeping the parts separate helps
ZBrush handle the data. The program is much better at
dealing with several medium-weight objects than just one
super-heavy 15-million polygon model.

5. In Figure 13.4, I show the progression of the construction
of the Formic from a head/neck/torso set of objects. I
progressively add arms, refine the shape, and then rough
in the final characters.

It is not my goal to sculpt out everything in high polygons;
I'm mostly interested in blocking out the overall form. This
gives me the freedom to brainstorm in 3D as I go along.

What I usually do after I rough everything out is combine
some of the primitive SubTools in a way that has an
anatomical sense such as head, torso, arms (then mirrored),
front leg, rear leg, and so on. I don't want to have dozens
of SubTools, but just a few combined.

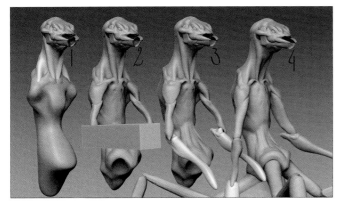

Figure 13.4 Adding other new geometries for torso, arms, and more.

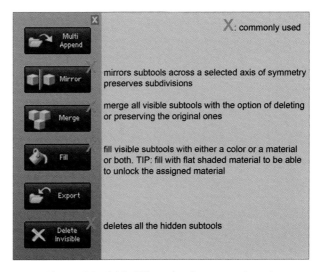

Figure 13.5 SubTool Master; functions commonly used.

5. I do all this SubTool editing using SubTool Master, which makes it easy to combine by using visibility, mirroring, subdivision levels, mass deletion, and more. See Figure 13.5.

TIP

The model is built like a wooden doll; every articulated section is a cube. The only topology tweak is adding some edges if the cube has become too skewed. This makes it easy to articulate the model, change the attachment points of the limbs, and mirror it to the other side.

6. After the whole thing is blocked out, I like to make general shape tweaks. I cannot do this if I keep the model separate because it's possible to edit only one SubTool at a time. I use Transpose Master to easily combine the whole thing in one SubTool and then separate it automatically.

I usually use Transpose Master to pose characters. Here I use it to tweak the shapes, and I almost exclusively use the Move Brush to make adjustments. See Figure 13.6. Figure 13.7 shows another view.

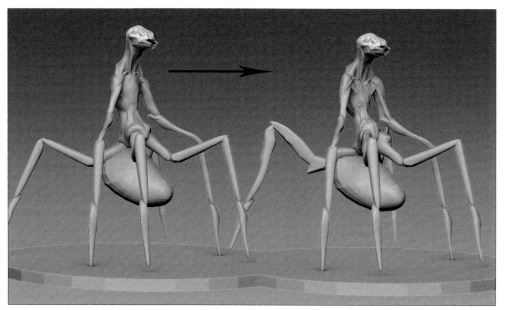

Figure 13.6   Combining the creature and tweaking the shape using the Move Brush.

TIP

The flow of the design allows you to create something with elegance and beauty. Each form has to flow to the other with some sort of rhythm. Try working in silhouette using a flat shaded material with a black color and deforming the model with big strokes of the Move Brush.

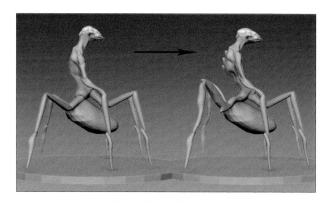

Figure 13.7   Different view.

NOTE

Every living creature has evolved through millions of years to perform its functions in the most efficient way possible. Keep this in mind when creating something brand new. You can do this when you brainstorm the design, but it's even more important to keep this in mind once the sculpture takes form.

Here in particular there's a creature that has to be able to adopt two different stances: an erect one and an ant-like six-legged one. Positioning the joints was quite tricky because I wanted the abdomen to be able to rotate from below to behind. I had to leave a space from between the rear set of legs to do so.

It's better to make functional design decisions before you begin your work because so much of the overall performance in animation depends on it.

7. I start defining the shapes. Controlling the way the surface is sculpted involves controlling how the sculpture is going to look. To control the surface during the development of the forms, I must have a clear idea of what each of the tools is going to do.

   I also consider how different shapes relate. If a shape is sitting on top of another, I keep a sensation of "depth" in the model. When sculpting, this happens all the time. I start sculpting the underlying shape and then add the upper layer as if I were working with clay.

The main tools I use are shown in Figure 13.8. However, I like to experiment with different ones and share tricks with other professionals. I'm always looking for more efficient techniques. I've tweaked my toolset quite a lot throughout the years, so I don't get stuck doing things one set way.

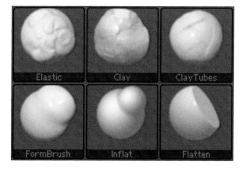

Figure 13.8   The main tools I use.

TIP

Hotkeys can be helpful to speed up sculpting. In particular, I use the Z button assigned to the Z Intensity slider with S assigned in default to the Brush Size slider.

To assign a command to a hotkey, press Ctrl+Alt and click on the button you want to assign the hotkey to. If you want the hotkey to make a slider pop up, click on the slider you want and then normally assign the key.

STEFANO DUBAY

8. I constantly refer to www.digimorph.org, which provides free X-ray 3D turntables of all sorts of animals. It's really the ultimate skeleton reference source. With those examples, it's easy to hybridize different animals creatively while still being grounded in reality. Animal skeletons are similar in some aspects to humans. With a little experience, it's not too complicated to learn to find similarities and use what is known of human anatomy in other creatures as well.

I start by sketching out a rough skeleton for my creature, focusing on the areas that have a lot of motion. (They have a complex layering of muscles to make the motion possible.) The shoulders are a great example of that, as are the hips.

A skeleton sketch also helps locate the correct attachment points for bone sockets.

Although it feels like overdoing it because most of what I do here will be covered by soft tissue, sketching the skeleton really helps me break up something complex as the anatomy of the creature.

A good skeleton also aids me in figuring out the alternate physiology of a creature. For example, here we have a humanoid torso attached to a double set of legs; the hip bone must be structured accordingly.

9. On top of the skeleton, when it's clear how the different bones relate and how their shapes are established, it's time to start adding muscles. Muscles originate from an attachment point and attach to an end point. They are tedious at the ends, and they bulge in the middle. They work like hydraulic pistons, by connecting on the articulated bone in a way that makes the motion possible. In other words, muscles are not just cool-looking bulging masses to make the model look good; they have to have a function, and this will define their structure. Muscles have to be added from the inside out.

The first ones to be added are deeper ones—the ones closer to the bones. Then the more superficial ones are added. The muscles form the surface of the body. This way it's easier to maintain a clear relationship between the different forms that compose the surface.

10. The final layer is the skin. Skin is like a layer of plastic wrap or wet paper on top of the forms of the muscles. It smoothes out the harsh transitions between the different layers of muscles and integrates them into one continuous, cohesive form. Skin, then, is susceptible to flexing, wrinkles happen in areas with a lot of bending or stretching and it behaves a lot like fabric would. If fat is present, it will be like a cushion (more or less lumpy) between the muscle and the skin. See Figure 13.9.

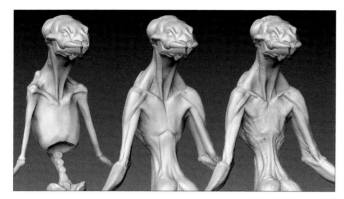

Figure 13.9 Developing the anatomy by layering skin and fatty tissue over muscles and bones.

TIP

A great tool to do that is the Clay Brush. Try to use it making a small circular motion at a low Z intensity (1 to 5), maybe with the addition of a noisy alpha, after the muscles had been sculpted. Think of it as brushing the surface of a plasteline clay sculpture with acetone.

11. At this point in the development of the creature, I decide to add antennae.

I try to look for extra references whenever I want to add something. It gives space for inspiration and helps to make the creature more grounded in reality.

Figure 13.10 shows a collection of antennae shapes I found online. Evolution came up with an incredible variety of shapes. There is no better master to learn from than nature!

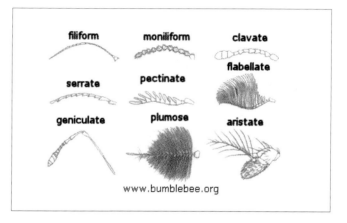

Figure 13.10 Reference found in books to refine the concept with detail elements.

STEFANO DUBAY

12. After I am finished with my secondary forms (primary forms are what are achieved when blocking in the model; secondary shapes are the more high-res sculpted features), I add a pass of tertiary forms with stencils. I don't rely on stencils to create anything important. They are image based; consequently, the way they affect the object is defined by the alpha used, not by the flow of the forms. See Figure 13.11.

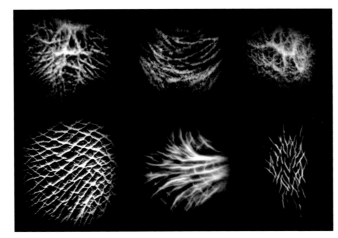

Figure 13.11 Alphas used in the final detail pass.

TIP

It is much better to sculpt as much as possible "by hand" and then use stencils to quickly dress up the surface and to give it a more organic and complex feel.

To alpha stamp, I use the settings shown in Figure 13.12.

Figure 13.12 Setting used to stamp alphas.

Figures 13.13 and 13.14 show the brushes and alphas, which are mostly used in different areas.

TIP

I do my alpha stamping on a layer, so I can easily use the Morph Brush to locally undo the stamp. This often happens when the stamp overlaps in a weird way or the surface looks dirty and needs refinement. It's also important to connect the different stamps by manually cleaning the surface a little, meaning connecting the crosshatches, building up some areas between the wrinkles and inflating the wrinkly areas.

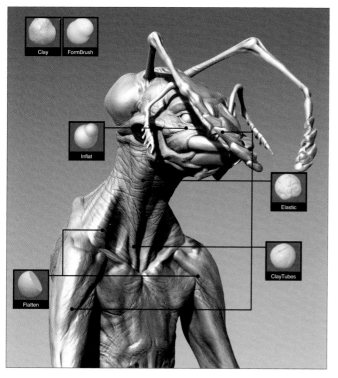

Figure 13.13 Breakdown of the brushes and alphas: front view.

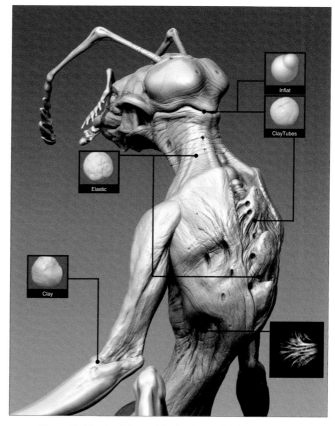

Figure 13.14 Breakdown of the brushes and alphas: back view.

STEFANO DUBAY

13. A trick I use with alpha stamping on "thin" objects (here I am stamping an alpha on the fangs) is to enable backface masking. An alpha project is used spherically to normalize the details to the surface. A drawback, though, is that once the projection "sphere" becomes too big, it hits, or reverses, the other backfaces. To avoid that, I use the BackfaceMask button (circled in red in Figure 3.15). The button is located in the Brush, Auto Masking drop-down menu.

There is also a slider called Backface Automasking Intensity (BackfaceMask and BackMaskIn) that I set either to 100 if I have my Alpha Brush in Zadd mode or to –100 if it's in Zsub. This automasking masks out subtraction or addition, respectively, to the surface. If you want to sculpt and nothing happens, it's probably because you forgot that BackfaceMask is on. Sometimes the result is better if the mask is inverted from what is obtained from the image.

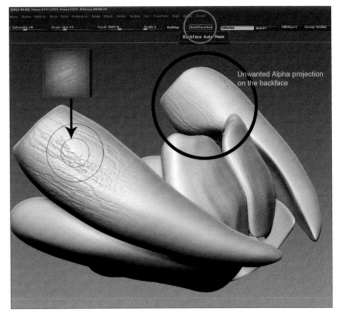

Figure 13.15   BackfaceMask to avoid having the alpha stamping spill on the rear faces of the object it's applied on.

TIP

For a more chiseled hard look, use the Flatten Brush with Clay Brush to randomly dig in the surface. Also, the Noise and Fracture Brushes help to mess up the surface.

TIP

Inflating a layer makes it easy to tweak the intensity of the first inflation.

Insights

Q&A

What motivates you or your work?

When I finished the university, I found myself struggling to find my place in the world, trying to find something that really moved me and made me feel like I was doing what I really wanted. Sometimes it's not easy to look within and listen to what your spirit tells you.

I am not an artist who has been drawing/painting since birth. I have other interests that tend to distract me from following a clear, linear path.

I have always thought of myself as more of a scientist than an artist. What my soul craves is expression. I need to make some part of myself get out from my daily daydreaming and into something I can touch and feel.

As my skills have become more robust and my objectives have become clear, I've learned to be patient. All artists want a magic wand to make their vision happen, but without patience, the art part doesn't occur.

Sometimes it's necessary to give your mind a break and just love who you are and what you do. Because ultimately you create art for yourself and not to impress others.

Who/what are your inspirations and influences?

The key to inspiration is sensibility. It isn't quite the mimicking of what's already out there in the world of art, but the observation of what's around. Inspiration happens to me in the form of symbols that sometimes pop in at the most improbable of times. After that, once the symbol is grasped, influence comes from the process of research and refinement of the idea.

Which artists do you admire? Why?

Every time somebody asks me about my influences, I feel overwhelmed by the answer. I seldom look at one specific artist. I can spend hours scouring the Internet for interesting things. Of course, the big names of the past always blow my mind. I recommend using the Google Art Project, which allows browsing of many great museums and zooming the canvases to a microscopic scale. I really like seeing the single strokes that developed the artwork. Also, DeviantArt.com and many other online forums are essential assets.

On the contemporary art side, I am really enjoying the work of Terryl Whitlatch and the way she seamlessly blends different creatures into one. I also love the work of Zdzislaw Beksinski and the realism movement.

Old painters and sculptors that I find inspiring are Rodin, Caravaggio, da Vinci, Michelangelo, and Botticelli.

When did you start using ZBrush?

I started playing with ZBrush when I read about version 2 in different magazines. I was just starting to polymodel then. ZBrush's impact on me has been huge!

What's your workflow? Do you create from scratch with ZSpheres or import geometry from another package to work on/develop?

I use Maya to polymodel. With it, I use a plug-in called NEX that simplifies the resurface process. I like the unified skin technology when I sketch. The only downside is the heaviness and messiness of the generated geometries.

STEFANO DUBAY

What are some of your favorite ZBrush features? How do you use them?

I really like the Unified Skin tool that works a little like voxels. I also use a lot of Morph Targets to erase a change on a section of the model and revert it to a previous state.

Are you using SpotLight to texture or for sculptural details? Please explain.

No, I'm not.

Are you using ShadowBox to make base meshes? How?

I use ShadowBox occasionally to block in shapes. I see lots of potential there!

What tools do you most often use to texture? SpotLight? Image Plane? Projection Master? ZAppLink?

I use ZAppLink, but I still paint most of my maps in Photoshop. I use ZAppLink for a first projection pass. I also sometimes base my colors on Polypaint and use Cavity and Occlusion masks as alphas for dirt maps and Subtle Color additions. I try to go lightly when I do so, keeping my color pass as unshaded as possible. Of course, when dealing with game models, I bake more of the lighting in my maps.

How do you use Best Preview Render for rendering your final image?

I use Best Preview Render (BPR) all the time now that it's available. The settings I usually use include the Create Maps buttons, Render, ZDepth, Shadow, Ambient Occlusion, and Alpha Mask.

I crank up the rays to the maximum, because it makes the calculation more accurate. I raise a bit of the resolution as well at times. The angle factor is also pretty important; it controls the spread of the shadows. In other words the closer the shadow is to the object that's casting it, the more focused it is going to be; while further out, it blurs. I reduce the blur slider to 2 if I want to blur it further, though I prefer taking care of that in Photoshop.

Are you using Photoshop overlay for your final image?

I composite the separate passes generated by the BPR in Photoshop. In other projects that are more illustration based, I heavily colorize the image with washes of color and then use that as a start point for a digital painting. I usually end up having hundreds of layers that I progressively flatten when I do that.

ZBrush lighting is much more complex than ever before. Do you use any of the advanced features? Which ones? Material generating?

I just use the directional light to create BPR shadows.

How do you make use of customizable tools in ZBrush?

I have a custom UI that I use constantly with my tools.

What are some of your time-saving tips when using ZBrush?

I make it easy to undo my work. Keeping layers and generating Z Morph Targets can be fundamental toward achieving a broad range of effects or simply deleting the surplus.

What advice do you have for artists working with ZBrush?

ZBrush is a tool that is a go-between with other software to create art. Treat it as such.

Resources

Links

- www.digimorph.org
- http://vimeo.com/22791048
- stefanodubay.blogspot.com
- digimorph.org
- zbrushcentral.com
- 3D.sk

STEFANO DUBAY

Contact
Stefano Dubay ▪ Hollywood, CA ▪ Stefanodubay@gmail.com
▪ www.4thvanishingpoint.com

Studio
Character sculptor at Disney Feature Animation

Education/Experience
Bachelor degree in mathematics

Client List
Gentle Giant Studios, Rhythm and Hues, Sony Pictures
Imageworks, Psyop Inc.

Hardware/Software Used with ZBrush
Hardware: i7 at 3GHz with GeForce GTX 460 video card,
128GB SSD main drive, Wacom Intuos 4 tablet

Software: Maya, Bodypaint, Xnormal, NEX, Photoshop

STEFANO DUBAY

Gallery

"Aztec Witch."

"Berith."

"Goddess."

"Goddess Close-Up."

STEFANO DUBAY

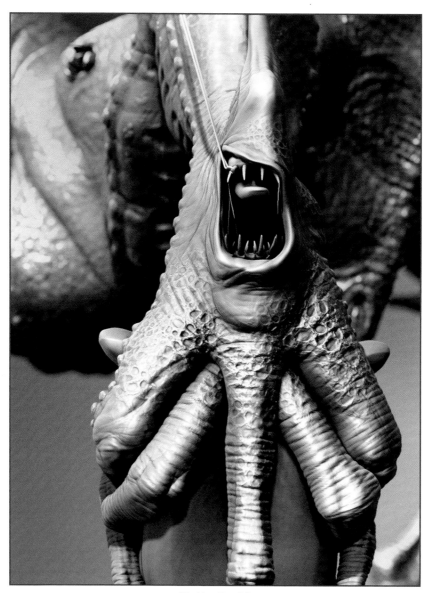

"Goddess Detail."

STEFANO DUBAY

"GHM."

"From *Land of the Lost* Movie."

INDEX

INDEX